IT'S PERFECTLY SAFE...

THE RULISON MATTER

MARILYN LUDWIG

It's Perfectly Safe... The Rulison Matter by Marilyn Ludwig
Copyright©2016 by Marilyn Ludwig

All rights reserved. No parts of this book may be used or reproduced in any manner whatsoever without written permission except in the case of brief quotations embodied in reviews.

Cover and interior designed by Ellie Searl, Publishista®

Colorado map in public domain
Map of Project Rulison area designed by Jon Ludwig
Photographs property of Ludwig family

ISBN-10: 0996742220
ISBN-13: 9780996742221
LCCN: 2016903668

Printed in the United States of America

ZAFA PUBLISHING
Downers Grove, IL

Also by Marilyn Ludwig

Miles: A Little Dog with an Eye for Friendship
co-authored with Kristin Ludwig
(2015)

Searching for Juliette
(2015)

"Lots of characters, both giving and politically conniving—innocent and dangerous. Good stories, skillfully interwoven. Complex. I was always happy to get back to reading it."—Sandra Duguid, author of *Pails Scrubbed Silver*

"Finally, a novel for young adults that respects its readers' intelligence. Ludwig provides a fascinating mix of history, politics, and language, all while unfolding an intricately wrought plot. Searching for Juliette will keep you guessing and (most importantly) make you think, in addition to being a rollicking good tale." —Susan O'Byrne, author of "Stephen King and the Monstrous Mother" from *A Casebook on Stephen King's IT*.

Haste Ye Back
(2015)

"In the rapidly growing genre of YA books, Marilyn Ludwig's mystery novels stand out for their fast-pace and great writing. Haste Ye Back is set in the British Isles and the flavor of the country is on every page, enticing the reader to want to see for herself. This is the perfect book selection for any reader, any traveler, of any age. I know I'll slip Ms. Ludwig's next book in my carry-on bag!" —Melinda Morris Perrin, author of *Prairie Smoke, Goldenrods, and Winterberries*.

"Marilyn Ludwig writes with love—love of the English language, love of youth, love for drama, and love for the cultural and historical landscape in which she places her stories and characters. Haste Ye Back is her newest book of page-turning suspense set in England and Scotland, and it is a feast of love! Marilyn has stored up many stories to tell, and I am so happy she is at last putting them down on paper to share with her readers. I look forward to her next book to add to the growing 'Marilyn Ludwig Collection' in my personal library." —Susan Throckmorton, author of *The Humply Rumply Beast: Poems and Papercuts*, and *They'll Be Back!*

The Secret of Kendall Mountain
(2016)

"Marilyn Ludwig's *The Secret of Kendall Mountain is* an exciting adventure novel set on a special train in Colorado's avalanche country, enjoyable and relevant to both young readers and adults. Ludwig's prose is fast-moving and easy to read, and her knowledge of the thoughts and emotions of teens and their families insightful. This novel will keep readers engrossed in an adventure in which the suspense does not stop until its dramatic conclusion." —Mardelle Fortier, Instructor at College of DuPage and author of *White Fire* and many poems and short stories.

"*The Secret of Kendall Mountain* is a wonderful story that readers of all ages will enjoy. The young heroes, who are quite believable and relatable, are called upon to perform a daring rescue and solve a lingering mystery against the backdrop of avalanche season in the Colorado mountains. The setting is beautifully described, and the suspenseful tale is well-told and sure to satisfy." —Mike Manolakes, author of *Variation Seven, Strange Times, Living in the Future,* and *Dying in the Past.*

For Braydon,
who listens and understands the magic of Anvil Points

In memory of our best Colorado friend,
Carolyn D. Love

and for Nancy

Aerial view of Anvil Points,
showing location of author's home

Author's home in Anvil Points

"Secrecy, once accepted, becomes an addiction."
—Edward Teller (1908-2003)

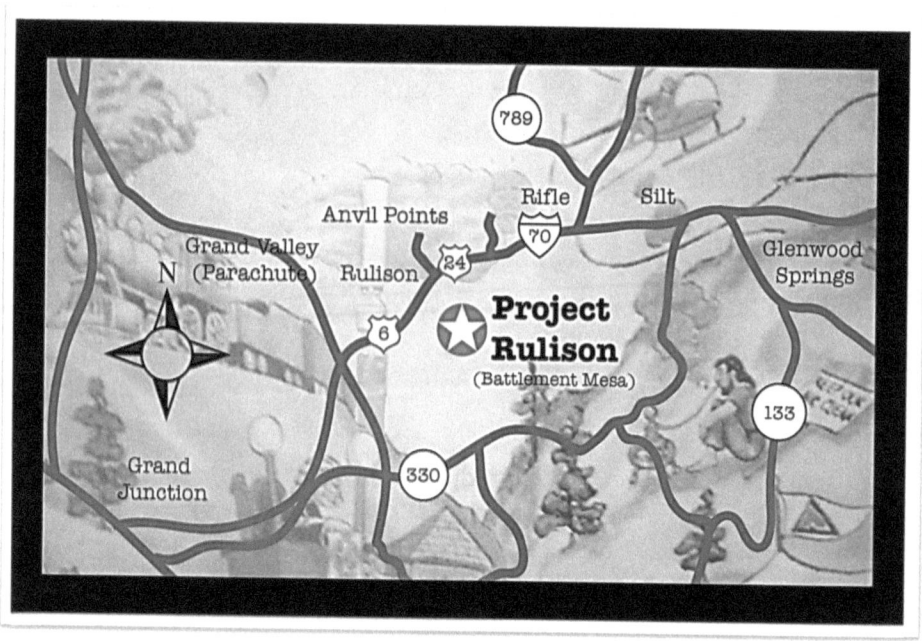

Designed by Jon Ludwig

Colorado

Prologue

Aunt Meg had fallen asleep again, physical therapy becoming almost more than she could bear. "You rest now," I whispered. "I'll be back."

But would I? This was my third visit to Margaret Shaw's new home at Mesa View, an assisted-living complex outside of Denver. Each time, she seemed more distant—less aware of my presence—and I doubted I'd return.

How old was she? Not much more than seventy, I thought, younger than many of my friends' relatives, but first a severe car accident had kept her confined to a wheelchair, and recently a series of strokes finished the job, draining all that was left of youth.

Aunt Meg wasn't my real aunt—more of an honorary one. She never married or had children of her own but was my grandmother's best friend and helped raise *her* children.

When she heard I was coming to Denver on a business trip, my mother insisted I visit the nursing home. "You're looking for advice,

Susan," she said. "I don't know anyone wiser than Aunt Meg. If you can only get her started, she has lots of stories to tell."

Well, I did want advice about Tim and me, so I tried again. "He's going to take that lobbying job—convincing Congress to lighten fracking regulations—and he wants me to go with him. I hate what he does, but I think I love him. Don't you think if he loved me enough, he'd give it up? What do you think I should do?" I didn't expect a response.

She seemed frozen in place. Had she even heard me? I bent over to kiss her goodbye. She gave a start—suddenly alert—looked into my eyes, and then spoke in the strong voice of someone healthier and much younger. "Sit down, dear," she said. "I must tell you a story."

She cleared her throat and began. "One suitcase. That was all that went with me from my old life to the new . . ."

Chapter One

"Okay, Dad, put the suitcase in the car. If I'm missing anything, I'll buy it there."

"Don't be so sure," Dad said. "I remember that place better than you do."

"I'll go to Sadie Eicher's store in Rulison." We grinned at each other, remembering the fiery old lady many people said was just plain crazy.

"Anything you need, Meggy, we'll mail later. We've already trusted the post office with your typewriter."

Unlike the rest of my family, Dad understood why I was going. Mom was so against it she had become impossible. My brother Todd, just turned eighteen, cared about his buddies and new driver's license. His only goal was to raise money to buy a car; he was not interested in his sister's future.

My college friends didn't understand either, as they prepared for their first teaching assignments—all local. Libby, my closest friend, would teach here in Des Plaines, at the elementary school where we first met. "I suppose it's too boring for you here," she said. "You must leave and have a grand adventure."

It wasn't like that. How could I explain? "It's more of a calling. A feeling. Ever since we left Colorado when I was ten, the mountains have been calling me back. I still dream about them."

Libby shook her head. "I don't know how you'll be able to live on that salary."

"I'll manage." I stopped trying. She would never understand. No doubt Libby and I would miss each other at first, but we would likely drift apart. I guess she was right about me. Staying in the same town, teaching at the same school, did sound boring.

Dad hauled the heavy case to the station wagon while I said goodbye to my lonely looking room. I had urged my mother to remodel it for herself. "An office, Mom, or just a place to store things?"

But Mom was certain I'd return and would want to find the room unchanged. "You were a child, Meggy. You don't remember what it was like. You'll be back—sooner than you think. I'm afraid this is the biggest mistake you've ever made."

Perhaps I should make mistakes. I had never been allowed to. Time to grow up. First thing—lose the childish nickname. You're Meg now, I decided. I saluted my Northwestern Class of 1969 pennant. It would be waiting for me if I returned.

Dad and I didn't speak on our way to Union Station. He concentrated on the traffic. But it was a comfortable silence. We never needed to talk much anyway. I was glad Mom and Todd were at work. Mom would have been too emotional and Todd, indifferent. This way was neater.

After parking the car, Dad opened his wallet and pulled out a fifty-dollar bill. "I'll send a little every week until you get your first pay check. Then you're on your own."

"Thanks, Dad." I'd saved some money over the summer, so I considered refusing his offer, but I wasn't stupid. Libby was right about the puny salary. Hers in Des Plaines was seven thousand a year, while mine was a little over five thousand. Less after taxes and things I didn't know about. Remembering that, I kept quiet when Dad paid for my train ticket.

"I'm proud of you, Meggy. Your mother is worried you might hear things out there that will bother you. But I said you've got a good head on your shoulders." A quick hug and Dad was gone.

I'd think about what he meant later. "All aboard," I said. I took my place on the train heading west.

Chapter Two

The stationmaster in Denver helped plan the next leg of my journey. "A few seats left on the Vista Dome. You're in for a treat. Just ask them to let you off in Rifle. A special stop, but they'll help out a pretty little lady like you."

"Thanks. I went to school in Rifle, and I've come back to teach."

"Fine town and good schools, I hear. Not many jobs to be had these days. You're lucky."

"Actually, I won't be teaching in Rifle. I'll be in the town just west of there—Grand Valley."

"Grand Valley? That's near Rulison, isn't it?"

What an odd question. Like saying, *Chicago, isn't that near Des Plaines?* Grand Valley was a metropolis compared to Rulison. "I'm surprised you've heard of it."

"Well, yes. Isn't that where . . . Oh, never mind . . . Just a rumor, I'm sure." The station master began checking his notebook. He was finished talking with the "pretty little lady." No matter. I needed to concentrate on what came next.

Soon I was a passenger on the famous Vista Dome train. "I'll just drink in all this scenery," I said to the server offering a beverage. She shrugged, as if to say it was too late in the day to be cute, before turning to a man who had pulled out his wallet. I returned to the all-encompassing window. The leaves on the cottonwood trees were turning yellow, creating the feel of fall. The sky was a clear, end-of-summer blue. How beautiful it was. In the distance, I spotted green mountains with white snow tops. Not my sand and red rock mountains yet, but I would see them soon.

As I told Libby, the mountains haunted me throughout childhood. The one-dimensional flatness of Illinois never seemed like home, so when I was officially an adult with a career, I applied—but was turned down—for a teaching position in Rifle. A higher salary and an apartment of my own would have been wonderful, but I accepted the position in Grand Valley as the next best thing. No apartments there were available, and I couldn't afford to buy a car and commute from Rifle. Thus, I would board with a family near the school—a husband and wife and their two teenage sons. In the few letters we exchanged, the woman, Mrs. Gower, seemed friendly.

The train approached Glenwood Springs, and I waved back at the whitewater rafters, rushing along with the Colorado River. What fun they were having. Back in pre-Salk vaccine days, during the height of the polio scare, I wasn't even allowed to go swimming. I promised myself I'd go whitewater rafting *and* swimming in Glenwood Springs' outdoor heated pool, the largest in the world. Then as the train made its way through the narrow, red—when not muted by shadows—Glenwood Canyon, reality became more interesting than daydreams.

"Best gather your belongings now, miss. The stop in Rifle will be a short one."

Rifle Depot was deserted and the ticket window closed. Sixteen years had passed since Dad and I had waited there to board the train for a trip to Denver—a dental emergency caused by too much candy. And it had been twelve years since we left Colorado for good. One day, I had been in my fifth grade classroom making plans for Halloween and almost the next we were gone, leaving most of our possessions behind. I never questioned it. I was a child. I obeyed my parents.

Five o'clock in the afternoon. A busy time in Chicago, but here in Rifle, everyone had gone home for dinner and rest. Too late to reach Grand Valley today, but I remembered the name of a hotel in town—the Old Midland. That would be my next stop.

Chapter Three

I AWOKE, SLUGGISH, UNCERTAIN, AND homesick. Back in Des Plaines today, my friends would throw a bridal shower for Elaine, who had had the good sense to become engaged to the first man who asked her. I thought her foolish at the time, but now . . . at least she knew what she was doing today.

Downstairs, the waitress took my breakfast order, and I asked, "Do you know how I can get to Grand Valley? A bus or a taxi?"

"No buses, miss, and I doubt you'll get a taxi on Sunday. But I wouldn't know. I don't live here. I come over from Silt." Silt was just east of Rifle, but she made it sound as if it were clear across the country.

"I do need to go there today. Any suggestions?" She didn't reply. Someone would be at the front desk at checkout time; I'd ask then.

Another night in Rifle was out of the question because of meetings in Grand Valley the next day. I hated to wait until 11:00 but guessed there was no choice. In the meantime, I'd take a walk around town to see what remnants of the past still existed.

Even now, Main Street Rifle resembled an Old West movie set, though an empty one, with most of the residents in bed or church. I was headed over toward 4th Street, wondering if my old school had been torn down, when I saw an elderly man walking his dog. A Saint Bernard. Our doctor used to have Saint Bernards. Could it be?

"Dr. Moore," I called out.

The man turned and smiled. The dog smiled, too. "Why, yes . . ."

He didn't recognize me, of course. I offered the dog the back of my hand, which instantly became soaked.

"I'm Margaret Shaw. I was your patient for years."

He looked me over. "Meggy?"

"Yes. I'm not surprised you didn't recognize me. I've changed."

"Oh, not so much. Prettier maybe, neater with your hair combed."

I laughed. He did remember. "My hair used to be a tangled mess."

"Such a long time ago. Are your parents and Todd here, too?"

"No, they're back home—in Illinois. There's just me."

"A vacation?"

I explained I was starting my first year of teaching in Grand Valley but seemed to be stuck in Rifle.

"Well, Meggy, you're stuck no longer. I've got to get Trixie home now and take care of a few matters. Come for dinner at one, and afterwards I'll run you out to Grand Valley."

I made a polite, half-hearted protest.

"No problem at all. Lovely day for a drive, and Rispa will be tickled to see you again. You did leave suddenly. We've always wondered about that."

"Dad got a job in Chicago," I said.

Dr. Moore made sure I remembered how to get to his house. One last lick from Trixie, and I continued my walk. It was good to reconnect with the kind doctor, and I was relieved to have such an easy way out of town. But his comment troubled me.

The way we left was strange and had become a painful memory. It had been Halloween night when I came home from Trick-or-Treating, soaked from the early season snowfall. Dad and Mom greeted me at the back door. "Good, you're home," Dad said. "We've got to move fast." I noticed then the suitcases in the hall.

"At least let her get out of these clothes, Chet." In my bedroom, Mom helped me out of my sodden costume. "No, don't put on your nightgown," she said, as I reached into the drawer.

"Why not? I'm sleepy."

She handed me Teddy for comfort and helped me into blue jeans and a sweater. "Daddy has been offered a wonderful job in Chicago. We're leaving right away."

"So soon?" But I was weary and only ten. I did what I was told.

Mom packed my clothes and told me to select one doll, one book and, of course, Teddy. Todd was only six, but his possessions filled most of the car. We left before daylight, never saying goodbye to Dr. Moore, my teachers, our neighbors, or my best friend, Loreen.

From where I stood on Main Street, I could see Anvil Points way off in the distance, although not the exact site of the government camp where we lived. Perhaps on the way to Grand Valley, Doc Moore would be willing to drive up the Anvil Points Road. But now it was time to check out of the Old Midland. The hotel agreed to hold my luggage at the front desk.

At 12:45, I collected my heavy suitcase and lugged it to the Moores' combination home and office near the old 4th Street School. Rispa didn't seem as delighted to see me as Doc Moore had predicted. I got a weak my-how-you've-grown greeting, but she had never really known me. I was just one of her husband's many patients, and a child at that. Her conversation now consisted mainly of questions—some making me uncomfortable. Who had been my father's employers after we left? Did my mother work? Did my father make much money? Well, maybe she wasn't that blunt, but that's what she meant. I was grateful when dinner was served, and I could concentrate on eating. I was returning from the bathroom when I heard a conversation clearly not meant for me.

"Meggy Shaw, back after all these years. What was her mother thinking?"

"Now, Rispa, you know Candy never had much say in that family."

"Then her father. How could he have let her come? Why Chet Shaw isn't in jail is beyond me."

"I'm wondering why she was hired—with Caroline Tucker on the GV school board."

"They say Caroline's husband never recovered from both the vanadium mill and the Anvil Points mines closing. I heard he just sits at home drinking beer and watching cowboy shows on TV."

"And plotting revenge, I'll bet. Something is wrong. Well, I brought her into the world, and it seems to me she turned out fine. I think I'll start making frequent trips into Grand Valley."

Dad had said I might hear things that bothered me. I wanted to ask for an explanation, but caution won. I backtracked and made a few noisy steps. They stopped talking.

Doc Moore smiled at me. "All set then?" I nodded and thanked Mrs. Moore for the meal.

"Any time." I didn't think she meant it.

Doc Moore placed my suitcase on the backseat of the station wagon, and we were on our way.

Chapter Four

Route 6 hadn't changed, but it appeared change was coming. Doc Moore said a new super highway would soon run parallel to it. "Be able to travel all the way to Denver in a few hours. Fine progress, but old Route 6 will be an access road for those of us who need it."

I was surprised to see a new vanadium plant in West Rifle. "I think my dad did some work at the old one."

"Indeed he did." Doc Moore sighed. "It closed in '58. People lost their jobs. Well, we'll see if they can make something of this new place. Lots of folks counting on it. How much do you remember about Grand Valley, Meggy?"

"Nothing much. Not the way I do Rifle and Anvil Points. But I call myself Meg now."

He nodded. "More grown up. Well, you'll like Grand Valley, Meg. Small, of course, but interesting history for a teacher. It's called the Home of the Rock that Burns."

"Why?"

"The old story goes that back in the late eighteen hundreds, a pioneer settled there and built himself a cabin with an oil shale rock fireplace."

"Uh-oh," I said, realizing where this was going. I remembered teenagers fooling around with oil shale and matches in Anvil Points. I knew what happened next.

Doc grinned. "Well, the Ute Indians warned him, but he wouldn't listen. He held a grand housewarming party and invited everyone, even the Utes, who wisely declined. Just had to test out his fireplace. The oil shale ignited, set fire to the cabin, and down it went. Fortunately, no one was hurt."

I might have commented, but we had come to a sign. "Oh, there's the Anvil Points road."

To my disappointment, he drove on past. "Let's save it for another time. Ethel Gower must be wondering what happened to you." Since we called her from the Moores' house, I knew Mrs. Gower wouldn't be wondering anything, but I let it go. He didn't want to take the detour and was doing me a huge favor already.

The drive from Rifle to Grand Valley was short. I never realized how dusty and drab the town was. A short main street with a few houses and small stores, a gas station, a couple of side streets with houses in need of repair—that was it. Yes, the rocky cliff backdrop was spectacular, but the community itself was dismal.

The Gower house was on a side street. I thought it must be one of the largest homes in town, vintage Victorian, with a wide, covered front porch, sadly needing a paint job. I was to discover that most of Grand Valley's houses did.

Ethel Gower made us welcome in her kitchen, which I suspected was her domain and, therefore, the most important room in the house. She was a tall, angular woman, almost completely gray, who looked used to hard work and was probably younger than she appeared. Doc Moore said goodbye, adding that he'd see me again soon.

Mrs. Gower graciously poured me a cup of coffee and explained that her family was new to Grand Valley. "Came a couple of years ago from

Denver. We needed a more peaceful place to bring up our boys." Something about the way she said "our boys" made me wonder if they might have been up to something not so peaceful back in Denver.

Ethel, as she insisted I call her, showed me my room. "I'll leave you to unpack. Come down to the kitchen if you want a snack or just a visit. We had our big meal after church, but I'm going to lay out sandwiches and such."

My bedroom was simple but adequate: a twin bed covered with a brown chenille spread, a dresser, a small wooden desk and chair, an empty bookcase, waiting to be filled. The walls were painted buff and decorated with Frederic Remington prints of the Old West. Not my taste, but they fit the room. The best feature was out the window—a breathtaking view of the Book Cliffs.

I unpacked in less than ten minutes and thought about going for a walk. First, I would stretch out on the bed . . . for just a few minutes . . .

Three hours later, I awoke with a start. The sun had set. I could forget about the walk. I could forget about meeting the rest of the Gowers, too. A note propped next to the coffee pot read, "Margaret, didn't want to disturb you. Hal, the boys, and I are at the Hall for a meeting about the project. Could be late. Eat the sandwiches and anything else you like. Ethel."

Ham on rye, a handful of potato chips, a pickle, and a bottle of 7Up—my first meal in my new home. I pushed aside some art supplies on the table and a hand-made poster with crude misspelled letters—SOON YOU WILL RADEATE BABY. Seemed childish for a teenager. I reached for the kitchen phone.

Todd answered on the first ring. "Mom, is that you?"

"No, Todd, it's me."

"Meggy! What's going on?"

"With what? How should I know? I'm in Colorado. Where are Mom and Dad?"

"I don't know. Not here. It's been bad since you left. Mom is mad at Dad, and Dad keeps saying everything is fine. But he isn't acting like things are fine. Mom says no one wants you there—that someone named Tucker is using you as a lure. Does that make any sense?"

"Not really. There's a Tucker on the school board."

"Well, they've both been acting weird. They weren't even here when I got up this morning. It's late, and I think I'm scared."

"Don't worry, Todd. We're talking about Mom and Dad. What could be wrong?"

"Okay, I guess I'm making something out of nothing. Do you want them to call you if—I mean when they get home?"

"No, I'll call back tomorrow." I noticed a click on the line—like someone was listening in. Not that we were saying anything important.

"You're sure everything is okay?"

"Of course it is. Call one of your friends and do something fun."

"Maybe I will. Thanks. Oh, wait. Mom's car just pulled in. Hold on. I'll go get her."

"No, just say I made it, and I'll call soon." No need for the phone bill to be too high, and there was that click again. Grand Valley must still have a party line. I shrugged. Just someone being nosy.

Chapter Five

Bright sunshine and a new day. Only 8 a.m., and I wasn't due for meetings until 9:30. I dressed quickly in my wrinkle-free skirt and drip-dry Ship 'n Shore blouse—no time to iron— and was grateful for a short, simple hairstyle that didn't need much fuss. I hurried downstairs, hoping to meet the rest of the family. Again, the kitchen was deserted, although sweet rolls and fruit were available on the sideboard, the coffee in the Corningware pot still hot. My spirits plummeted, remembering Mom's words. "You'll be lonely, Meggy. You won't know a soul. They can be very insular if you weren't born and raised there. It was different in Anvil Points. We all came from somewhere else and knew we wouldn't stay long. You won't have transportation. Probably not even a decent market in town. What will you do when you're not teaching?"

"I'll be part of the Gower family," I replied. But that wasn't going to happen. Ethel had been welcoming—to a paid boarder.

As I ate my solitary breakfast, I thought about Todd. He hadn't sounded so unsure of himself since he was eight-years-old and had come to me for everything. I'd call later, but he was probably back to his old self by now. A knock on the door chased away the lonely, worried thoughts. Someone to talk to was what I needed.

To my surprise, a young woman entered and headed straight for the coffee pot. "Oh, hi. You're Margaret Shaw, right? I'm Carrie. Carrie Kimberly. Doc Moore called this morning and said you might need a friend about now."

"Doc was right."

"We're heading in the same direction. I teach at GV, too, but I'm an old-timer. This is my second year. I survived—somehow—and so will you." A grin softened her words.

"I don't even know where the school is," I said, "or the Gowers."

"Could be Ethel's day to volunteer at the library. Hal and Artie must be at the mill by this time, and Freddy is helping pump gas at the filling station." Carrie noticed the rejected poster. "Honestly . . . And it's our job to teach them to spell."

"Do you know what it's about?"

"Project Rulison? Should be the main topic of conversation all week. Oops! Getting late. Let's get a move on."

Hastily, I rinsed off my dishes and stood them in the drain board. I started to turn the latch on the back door, but Carrie stopped me. "Don't bother. You're from back East. No one locks doors around here, Margaret."

"Meg."

"Cute. Suits you. I'm glad you're here. I need a friend."

"Me, too."

"Speaking of friends, Doc Moore said to tell you that someone you'll remember lives here in Grand Valley now. Loreen Brackett. She married Will Brackett. Don't know what her maiden name was."

"Really? Loreen Woods? We were best friends. I can't believe I'll get to see her again."

Carrie made a face. "She doesn't seem your type somehow."

I just smiled. Loreen used to be exactly my type, and the prospect of two friends in town cheered me considerably.

The school was only a few short blocks away, though not on the main road. I should have no trouble walking even in terrible weather. I must have exclaimed when I saw the building because Carrie, who had turned quiet, came to life again. "Nice, isn't it?"

"It certainly is." The school was huge. One side looked as if it had been around for a while, but the other was a new addition. I learned later it was actually two schools—the high school was housed in the newer side, and the grade school in the older. The grounds were beautiful—truly like a park—and the Book Cliffs leading to Anvil Points provided the backdrop. "It's larger than I expected."

"Well, yes," Carrie said, "especially since we have only twenty grade school students this year. But one thing you've got to know about us Parachute people is that we live in hope."

"Parachute?"

"The old name for Grand Valley. They changed it in the early nineteen hundreds. There's a group in town trying to get it changed back to Parachute."

Strange name, but it didn't seem important. "Twenty students? That's it?"

"As I said, we live in hope. We're always thinking some fine opportunity is going to come along, bringing jobs with large paychecks and more residents to put more taxes into the GV coffers. Happens a lot. A mining or gas company moves in, and everyone gets excited and starts building. Then the company changes its mind and leaves, and we're stuck with things like this." She gestured toward the school and sighed.

The town obviously needed money, and now they had one more teacher to pay. "I'm surprised they hired me. Do they really need another teacher?"

Carrie gave me a sharp look before answering. "We wondered about that. What made you think of applying here?"

I shrugged. "I missed the mountains, and I wasn't hired in Rifle." The truth was I didn't apply until invited to do so by the Grand Valley Board of Education. They must have heard about me from someone in Rifle. A letter was sent to the placement bureau at my college. I responded immediately and was overjoyed when my acceptance came almost by return mail.

Carrie opened the front door. "You do know that two of our students are the Gower boys?"

"But they're teenagers."

"Happens here. Not bright enough to move over to the high school. We do what we can until they're old enough to drop out or get drafted." I looked at her in dismay. She laughed. "Don't worry. You get used to it."

One of Carrie's acquaintances waiting in the hall beckoned to her, and she nudged me over and introduced the school secretary. I met the rest of the staff in the teachers' room: Mrs. Arnold, who taught science and arithmetic, and Miss Winn, art and music. Carrie and I would divide up the students and teach social studies and language arts.

Mr. Owens, the principal, addressed the group. "Welcome to another year at GV. Let me introduce Miss Margaret Shaw from," he looked down at his clipboard, "Illinois. I'm sure you'll all help her get settled." He reviewed his papers. "Miss Shaw, I'm assigning you Room Ten. You have a few hours now to make your plans and decorate your rooms before you take your lunch break." He gestured toward a tray of apples and doughnuts. "I see the PTA has provided refreshments. Miss Winn, please send them a letter of appreciation." Miss Winn smiled and nodded. All that sugar meant I would run out of energy fast, and there didn't seem to be a cafeteria for lunch.

Mr. Owens continued. "As you know, orientation and various meetings will take place at Rifle High tomorrow through Thursday. If you need more time in your classroom, the building will be open all today and Friday. On Friday afternoon, of course, we'll meet in the town hall to learn how to do our part for the project and to make early dismissal on the tenth go as smoothly as possible. Working together, I'm sure we'll have a successful year." He gathered his papers and bustled out of the room.

Meetings in Rifle? How was I to get there? And that word "project" again. "What project?" I asked.

Mrs. Arnold sneered at me. "What indeed?" She stormed from the room.

Miss Winn shook her head. "Don't worry about Ruth, Miss Shaw. She gets grumpy sometimes. I'll show you your room. I'm next door in eleven."

"I go the opposite way," Carrie said. "I'm in fifteen, and Ruth thirteen. You didn't bring a lunch. I did, but it's nothing special. Let's go to Hannah's Sandwich at noon, and we'll see about clearing up some of your confusion."

I nodded my thanks and followed Miss Winn.

Room 10 was barren: a few tables, an old wooden teacher's desk and chair, and ten desks. "If you need more art supplies for your bulletin boards, come see me." Miss Winn gave a half smile and left me alone.

Did I have *any* supplies? There weren't many books: uninviting tattered classics, a set of dated World Book Encyclopedias, and about twenty dictionaries. I opened the coat closet and found large rolls of paper on a shelf. I could cover the bulletin boards, but then what? No college class or student teaching experience had prepared me for this unfriendly room. I searched through the desk drawers for a curriculum guide, but the drawers were empty, except for a stapler, a pair of scissors, and an old Hershey Bar. I decided to find Carrie.

I peeked into Miss Winn's room. A wonderland of cheap cardboard cutouts covered her bulletin boards, but at least the room was colorful. Carrie displayed handwriting and phonics charts, a guarantee that kids like the Gower boys would be counting the days before they could legally quit.

Carrie looked up from her desk. "Meg, how is it going?"

"Slow. Is there any kind of curriculum I should follow?"

"Of course. Nothing in your room?" I shook my head, and she took a yellowed-with-age, tattered folder from a drawer. "Borrow this until you get your own copy. The master is in the office, but I'm not sure if the ditto machine is fixed yet."

At least they had one. "What about textbooks? I don't have any."

"They must all be in here. We can divide them up later."

I didn't respond. I should have, but I just stood there staring stupidly at her, wondering if anyone intended to help me.

"Until lunch, then," Carrie said. "Better get back to work. Owens may do a walk-through at noon, and he'll expect to see a lot done."

Maybe the curriculum guide would help me figure out what supplies I needed. Chalk. I'd forgotten to ask Carrie for some, so I poked my head into a classroom on the way back. "Excuse me, Mrs. Arnold. May I borrow a piece of chalk? There aren't any in my room."

"You'll have to requisition some," she said, not even looking up from the newspaper she was reading. "I need every piece I've got."

What an unpleasant person. She could be attractive if she replaced the scowl with a smile and wore a little makeup. And that short, straight-with-bangs look was not right for her. Well, I didn't have time for her problems. I had enough of my own.

Back in Room 10, I covered the boards with butcher paper and added blank sheets of colored construction paper. As uninspired as it was, I preferred my efforts to Miss Winn's and Carrie's. At least I'd created space for students' work.

I sat at my desk, put my head in my arms, and waited for noon. I wanted to go home.

Chapter Six

"They're exploding a nuclear bomb in Rulison next week!" I pushed aside my egg salad sandwich. "That's the project? You're joking."

"No joke," Carrie said, "but it will be buried underground. We won't feel the blast."

"Not feel a forty-kiloton nuclear bomb?"

"As I said, Meg, it will be deep in the ground. Perfectly safe."

"Which is why we'll have early dismissal?"

Carrie sighed. "I wish I understood the science behind it. We've been told they're going to blast the natural gas out of the rocks—release it to form a well so we can pump it easily. Grand Valley needs jobs."

"They're going to bomb Rulison so Grand Valley can have jobs." I wondered what Sadie Eicher thought about it. Perhaps the old woman who owned the store in Rulison was no longer there.

"Not where the houses are, of course. Out on Battlement Mesa. The AEC—that's the Atomic Energy Commission—will explain all about it at the meeting on Friday."

"Then I suppose I'll have to wait." I tried to eat but was almost numb with disbelief. "I'm surprised I haven't read about it. Even in Chicago, I should have heard something." A bomb more powerful than the ones that destroyed Hiroshima and Nagasaki didn't deserve even a mention on the back pages of the Chicago Tribune?

"The government must not want to start a panic. It is hard for people to understand. Listen, it's the government. They know what they're doing. Let's change the subject. You must have other questions—about school."

I did, although it was hard now to think about anything else. "I never knew about the meetings in Rifle," I said. "I don't have a car. How am I to go back and forth each day?"

"Oh, my, that is tough. It's hard around here without a car."

She hadn't made it easy. "Could I go with you?"

Carrie shook her head, seeming more interested in finishing her milkshake than in helping me. "I'm sorry, but I'm driving to Rifle this afternoon—to stay with my cousin until after the meetings Thursday. I hate getting up early, and she lives near the high school."

"What about getting your classroom ready for next week?"

Carrie laughed. "Nothing to it. I'm all set. Wish I could help. Why don't you ask Ruth and Effie—that's Miss Winn—if you can go with them? I don't know, though; there may be a load of stuff in Ruth's car. She's leading some of the meetings."

"I'll figure something out," I said.

She stood. "I've got to go home and pack. You leave the tip, and I'll do it next time. Oh, almost forgot. How about I teach the younger children—five through ten—and you take the older ones?"

"Fine," I agreed, although I had no idea if it were fine or not. Most of my training had been geared toward the younger grades. Appetite gone, I pushed the rest of my meal aside.

Back in Room 10, I read over the curriculum guide. I doubted that any of the suggested books, even if I had them, would help me teach older students. I needed those meetings in Rifle. Gathering my courage, I went looking for Mrs. Arnold and Miss Winn, but no one remained except the secretary. After packing the guide and a few textbooks from Carrie's room, I left the building.

I wanted Dad. Hannah's Sandwich Shoppe had a phone booth, so I returned there and called home collect. But the phone rang and rang until the operator cut in stating the obvious. Before leaving the booth, I jotted down some numbers from the phone book, just in case—a taxicab company and the Rifle YMCA. I hoped Ethel would offer better suggestions.

My hopes were dashed by another note in the kitchen, saying the family would be late getting home that night. "I'm sorry we keep missing each other," Ethel wrote. Mom was right; I was nothing more than a paid boarder. I thought briefly about contacting the Moores. Doc might have offered me a room, but Rispa would not want me. Grow up, I told myself. You wanted independence, and now you've got it.

I called the cab company and then the Y, reserving the cheapest room they had for three nights. Then I wrote my own note, explaining the situation, and propped it next to the coffee pot. Upstairs, I re-packed my suitcase, feeling foolish using such a large bag, but it was all I had.

What followed were the three loneliest days of my life, as I went from meeting to meeting in a daze. No one was unkind—except Ruth Arnold, who snubbed me—but the other teachers were wrapped up in their own concerns. I never saw Carrie and wondered if she had skipped the whole thing.

Some of the sessions were helpful, but most of them didn't apply to my situation—a poorly supplied classroom and a complete lack of understanding of what I was supposed to do. I heard varied opinions about the Rulison Project—most were positive. A successful outcome meant job security— new residents and more students to teach. We were told that before leaving school the day of the blast, we should move the desks away from the windows and remind the students to stay outside until they were certain the test was over. I wanted to ask why—if we weren't in danger—but didn't feel comfortable saying anything.

Later, I shopped for school supplies at the Rifle ten-cent store, even though I resented spending my own money. Perhaps it was something all beginning teachers did. I ate at inexpensive restaurants and at night, in my room, wrote out a few tentative lesson plans and made posters for the bulletin boards. I had a knack for drawing cartoons, and some of my posters were clever.

Each night, I phoned home, reversing the charges. But no one ever answered. I started to worry and called Ethel to see if Dad or Mom had been in touch, but they hadn't. She apologized for my circumstances and said she looked forward to seeing me on Thursday. By then, I no longer looked forward to anything.

Chapter Seven

Friday morning, I put the finishing touches on my bulletin boards. Sherlock Holmes holding a magnifying glass was "Searching for his Goals." I rolled little shelves of corrugated cardboard and stapled them to the board, creating the appearance of a library, and placed a few of the tired, tattered classics—*Black Beauty, Heidi, Tom Sawyer*—on them. Next to this odd bookcase, my cartoon judge held up his gavel and said, "Don't Judge a Book by its Cover." Not great bulletin board art by Northwestern standards, but certainly a huge improvement over what hadn't been there a few days before.

Carrie came shortly before 4:00. I wanted to ask her where she'd been the past three days, but it wasn't any of my business. She went around the room, silently examining my decorating efforts without comment. "Ruth and Effie will walk with us," she said finally. Ruth and Effie. I would continue calling them Mrs. Arnold and Miss Winn until they invited me to do differently.

The Hall was located in the police station, just a large room with a platform stage. A crowd, for Grand Valley, had assembled already. Mrs. Gower, who was talking to a group of women, rushed over, grabbed my hands, holding them tightly, as if to transfer some of her nervous energy onto me.

"We keep missing each other," she said. "I'm so sorry we were gone again last night when you came home." She nodded at Carrie. "I knew you two would hit it off. Such a lot of work to do—shopping, room preparations . . . One of the men from the AEC will be boarding with us. He and Hal knew each other back in Denver. Supper is at five-thirty, and we're counting on you being there to meet everyone."

"Thanks. I'll be there."

"You're family now, Margaret."

"Meg," I said.

"Better find a seat, Meg." She patted my shoulder and returned to the women. I felt more included but wasn't fooling myself. I wasn't family. Mine was in Illinois, where more and more I wished I could be.

While there were plenty of seats in the first few rows, Carrie led me to a place in the middle. I saw why in a few minutes when eight men wearing dark gray business suits came into the room and took the front row.

"Government," Miss Winn, who told me I should call her Effie, said. The name suited the wisp of a woman. Twiggy thin, with fluffy blond frosted hair and a striped shirtwaist dress, she seemed determined to look young—or at least way younger.

Grand Valley's mayor took the platform, introducing the representatives from the AEC. After polite applause, each man took a turn saying why Project Rulison was going to be a great thing: more jobs, cheap natural gas, less dependence on foreign countries, and on and on. All good things, of course, but after a while the men sounded the same, so I stopped listening.

Finally—"Are there any questions?"—the audience erupted.

"What about my peaches? They're ripening now. You gonna pay me if I lose my crop?"

"*Crop failure is unlikely, but you may file for compensation if you have proof that the project caused it.*"

"My farm depends on watering. Won't the river be polluted?"

"*Scientists have determined that won't be an issue.*"

"What about radiation?"

"*The explosion will take place underground.*"

"What about fallout?"

"*Again, the explosion will take place underground. No one will be affected above the surface. It's perfectly safe.*"

"Won't we all get cancer?"

Chuckles. "*Of course not!*"

The officials seemed condescending and arrogant, answering every question with these evasive non-answers. Where were the reporters? I didn't see anyone with so much as a notebook.

I started to raise my hand, but Effie forced it down. She nodded to where Mr. Owens was sitting and shook her head. I understood. The principal did not want his teachers involved in controversy. My question—why did we have to push the furniture away from the windows and go outside if there wasn't going to be an earthquake—seemed reasonable, but no one asked it. Perhaps I would at dinner. Correction—supper in Grand Valley.

After the meeting ended, the men hurried out the rear exit. Outside in front, a few people were picketing and holding up signs:

Kill Nature for Gas!

Soon You Will Radiate, Baby! Radiate was spelled correctly on that sign.

We're Going Nowhere! was held by a woman I recognized. Ancient and withered, but it was she. "Sadie! Sadie Eicher!"

She scowled. "Go way. I don't know you."

"Meg Shaw. Meggy. Remember? You gave me cherry lollipops when I was little. We used to shop at your store."

"Shaw!" Sadie spat. "Take my land, will you? I'm not going nowhere. Go way, Shaw!"

Carrie pulled me away. "Come on, Meg. She's crazy. Everyone knows that." I did know it, but Sadie's reaction shook me anyway.

"Are they taking people's land, Carrie? Did they take Sadie's property from her?"

Carrie shrugged. "Who knows? Her house is just an old shack." She added that she had to get home to her mother. I knew nothing about Carrie's life. I wondered if this was her fault or mine.

Back at the Gowers', I offered to help Ethel with supper. "Yes, and let's chat before Mr. Jeffreys and the others come." Mr. Jeffreys must be her husband's friend.

I tossed the salad while she prepared the meat sauce for her spaghetti, which smelled divine. Ethel said there were plenty of supplies in the refrigerator for making sandwiches and to just take whatever I needed each day. "And I go to the A & P in Rifle every Friday morning. Give me a list if you have any special requests." How about a car? I thought, knowing I would be stranded in Grand Valley if Friday morning was her only shopping day.

"That is so kind of you, Ethel," I murmured, and searched for something else to say. I thought the kitchen seemed different—perhaps just because the art supplies had been removed. "The sign is gone. The one that said we will radiate. Whose was it?"

She gave a weak laugh. "Oh, just one of the boys'—probably Freddy's. He has the hardest time spelling, but it could have been either of them."

"They're against the test?"

"That's hard to tell. Artie loves to defy his father. He's fourteen, a difficult age. Freddy is sixteen."

I gave an inward sigh. Both boys were way too old for my class, but this wasn't the time to talk about it. I returned to a different dangerous topic. "What do you think, Ethel? Do you think it's a good idea for the government to set off a nuclear bomb on Battlement Mesa?"

Ethel wiped her hands and sat across from me. "Makes it sound awful when you put it that way. Well, they say it's perfectly safe buried underground, but I don't know. I'm a little scared about the whole thing. What if they're wrong?"

What indeed? "But your husband thinks they should do it?"

"Oh, yes. That's one of the reasons we moved here. Hal thinks it will mean a better job for him, and he's got a lot of respect for Walt Jeffreys. Hal thinks anything Walt says goes." She stood. "We best get cracking. Would you set the table?"

"Of course."

Then it was time to freshen up for dinner. At the top of the stairs, someone was singing in a rich, male voice, twanging in accompaniment on a guitar. I grinned at the words.

> *So you say your cows are dying*
> *And you're feeling sickly, too,*
> *That thick gook in the water—*
> *You think it looks like glue.*
>
> *But relax my friends, just listen*
> *While I explain it all anew.*
> *'Cause don't you know?*
> *Haven't you heard?*
> *The bomb's perfectly safe for you.*

It sounded like something by Tom Lehrer, although I had never heard it before. I knocked on the closed door, and the music stopped.

"Come in." The voice was grumpy; still, an invitation. A boy, probably Artie but hard to tell, with hair too long by Grand Valley standards, was sprawled, legs askew, on a vinyl swivel chair. He spun around, still holding his guitar. "Oh, I thought you were Dad." He swept brownish hair out of his eyes. The hairdo might have been an attempt to hide an emerging crop of acne.

"I don't think he's home from work yet. I'm Meg. Meg Shaw."

"You mean Miss Shaw, because you're my teacher."

"Starting Monday, anyway. Great choice of songs. Did Tom Lehrer write it?"

"I don't think so." But Artie smiled. Somehow I'd pleased him.

"I take it you're not in favor of the project."

"Hell no!" He waited for my reaction.

I laughed. "All things considered, an apt comment, Artie. Or are you Freddy?"

"I'm Artie, and you're different than I expected."

"So are you. You have talent."

"I could use some lessons, but I won't get them here. And the GV music teacher is a dud." He embraced his guitar and began singing again.

> *So the fish float to the top*
> *And seem to have turned all blue,*
> *Your potato crop is ruined—*
> *Not even good for stew.*
>
> *But relax my friends, just listen*
> *While I explain it all anew.*

I joined in. *'Cause don't you know? Haven't you heard? The bomb's perfectly safe for you."*

"You're not bad," he said.

"And you're wonderful—and probably smart. Why aren't you going into high school?"

"Someone's got to keep Freddy company." Downstairs, a bell rang. "Supper." Artie put the guitar into its case. "Time for you to meet Dad's first choice for son—the amazing Walter Jeffreys. Or did you already meet him at the Hall?"

I admitted the men all looked alike to me. "A sea of dark suits."

"All spouting the same party line," Artie said. "Well, let's go. Being late for a meal is a crime in this household."

"I'd like to talk more sometime," I said.

"Sure."

The possibility of a friend, even if he were only fourteen.

It was a man's world at the dinner table—at least it was that night. I might have been offended at being overlooked if I hadn't grown used to it, and if I weren't so hungry. Ethel hustled back and forth to the kitchen bringing replenishments. I don't think she ever sat down. Both Hal Gower and Walt Jeffreys were cordial enough when we were introduced, but clearly they were delighted to be in each other's company and had much to discuss: people they both knew and all of the exciting prospects for jobs once natural gas became an easy drill away. Walt seemed to be in his late twenties—good looking in an academic way, a way that appealed to me. He was at least six-feet tall, with light brown hair that would have been curly if allowed, and dark, intense, brown eyes. His academic appearance might have been due to his wire rim-framed glasses. He could be worth knowing—if he ever looked my way.

Artie kept his head down and ate as if he wanted to distance himself as much as possible before heading back to his room. If his failure in school were caused by his reluctance to leave his older brother behind, we had a problem. As his teacher, "we" was the correct word to use. Freddy Gower resembled his father in that he was fair, large, overweight, smiley, and amiable. Unlike his father, Freddy was visibly retarded, a word we used freely in those days. I thought it likely he had Down Syndrome, and I wished I knew more about the condition. I doubted

Freddy cared about Project Rulison. He would go along with whatever pleased Artie, whom he obviously adored.

Someone said my name. "Sorry, I was lost in thought."

Hal Gower laughed. "Not surprising. You've had a busy couple of days in unknown territory."

"Not completely unknown," Ethel said. "Meg lived in Anvil Points from the time it first opened until 1957."

"How interesting!" Walt finally noticed me. "I'd love to talk with you about it sometime."

"I was just a kid." What a clever response, Meggy, I thought, kicking myself. That will surely keep him interested.

"You'll have plenty of time to talk," Hal said. "Walt is staying with us until the test is over. You're like a member of the family, my boy."

Artie winced, Freddy nodded happily, and Ethel sat expressionless. Something might have been bothering her. A strange assortment of people made up this family. Perhaps that was true of all families, including mine. Especially mine, I thought, wondering what in the world was going on with them.

Over dessert, Walt invited me to take a drive the following day and asked if I could suggest a destination. "How about Green River?" I named a town in Utah that was also the title of a popular protest song. What was it about the man that made me say the wrong things? But I had the pleasure of hearing Artie choke on his 7Up. Walt's eyes twinkled, though, suggesting that he, too, had caught the reference. I would be more careful not to underestimate him.

"A little far for tomorrow, especially since I'll be driving the company car. How about Anvil Points, and then maybe up to Rifle Falls?"

"Really? Oh, thank you so much!" Perhaps I sounded overly eager, but I didn't care. Soon I'd see my beloved mountains again!

Chapter Eight

September 6, Saturday

THE BOYS STILL ASLEEP AND Hal, long gone—Walt, Ethel, and I feasted on our pancakes. "Does Hal work Saturdays?"

Ethel nodded. "Sometimes. He is in Rifle now meeting with the mayor."

"That's right," Walt said. "Mayor Park's truck company won the contract for Project Rulison."

"You mean his truck is delivering IT?"

Walt grinned. "It?"

"You know—the bomb."

"Oh no," Ethel said, refilling our coffee. "Lester's trucks will haul in the rigs and whatnot."

"Rigs?" I didn't understand any of this.

"The crews will need them in order to drill the hole."

"The hole."

"Eight thousand, four hundred and thirty feet deep and just fifteen inches wide," Ethel said. "I could recite those figures in my sleep."

"How will it get here then? Thin Man or Skinny Boy or whatever we're calling this one."

"I don't think we've given it a name," Walt said. "The bomb will come from Los Alamos in an armored truck—maybe tomorrow or the next day. Security is pretty tight."

I must have made a face, for Walt rushed to assure me. "Many precautions have been taken. It's part of Operation Plowshare."

"Plowshare?"

"Using nuclear weapons for peacetime purposes. All that natural gas is trapped in the shale formations. We need it for fuel—for heating and cooling and driving our cars. For Ethel's fine meals and manufacturing and electrical power, and so much more." Walt glowed with enthusiasm. "And it's clean burning; won't pollute the planet the way coal or oil will. You and Art might want to sing about that."

"Operation Plowshare." I recalled my long ago Bible School days. "And they shall beat their swords into plowshares, and their spears into pruning hooks." Ethel joined me on the last line. "Nation shall not lift up sword against nation; neither shall they learn war anymore."

"Isaiah 2:4," she said softly. We exchanged looks, mentally sharing the irony.

Once the trip to Anvil Points began, I lightened up, though, and started to feel something almost foreign. I struggled to name it. Happiness. For the first time since I left home, I was happy. Walt was fun and funny and caring, as well as good-looking. It was such a relief not to be lonely. All of the problems still existed, but maybe I could take a break from them.

Walt asked about my teaching position, and I confessed how ill prepared I felt—in spite of the orientation at Rifle High. "The meetings were interesting but didn't seem to apply to our circumstances at GV."

"Having so few students should help some."

"But such an age range." I explained my concerns about Artie—deliberately doing poorly so he would not be promoted into a grade higher than his older brother.

"So that's what's going on. Back in Denver, Hal told me he was worried Art was becoming involved with hippies."

And there it was—one of my pet peeves. "Hippies. You mean young people who wear their hair long and actually care about something other than themselves?"

"Whoa! Didn't mean to set off the bomb so early. Where is that coming from?"

"Sorry. It just gets me mad when people lump others—especially young people—into one group. Are they talking about the youth who are involved with drugs and gangs, or do they mean those who understand we have no business in Viet Nam, or that we shouldn't be destroying our planet?"

Walt stopped the car and gave me a sharp look. "There's a lot going on under that cute hairdo, isn't there?"

"Sorry I got so emotional," I said, but I didn't like the personal comment. What did my hair have to do with my convictions?

Another scrutinizing look from Walt. We didn't speak again until we started up the Anvil Points Road, and I saw my dream of twelve years come true. The peaks and points were still majestic and cruel, but I also found them nurturing because I had been so happy and free there. I gazed at the faraway switchback roads, cutting their way up into the mines and greeted Big Boy Mountain as if it were an old friend I wished to embrace.

"Where did you live, Meg?" Walt asked, after a long silence. I did like that about him. He seemed to know when to talk and when to keep still.

"Right there." I pointed to the first house in a large circle of prefabricated homes, all abandoned. "Some of the houses are gone, but that one was ours."

Walt climbed the four rickety steps to the front door, which opened to his touch. "I'm surprised it isn't locked."

Even in my dreams I never imagined I would be inside again. "It's smaller than I remember. Everything is, except the mountains."

"Things do look larger to a child." Walt walked around the living room, examining a few walls. "It seems structurally sound. Which was your room?"

I showed him my back bedroom, with its view of Big Boy Mountain. "Sometimes we children would hike up there in the late afternoon to greet the men coming home from the mines."

"What an ideal place to grow up."

The conversation had been all about me. I should change that. "Where are you from, Walt?"

"From all over." Was he evading the question? I must have looked skeptical, for he said, quickly, "Really. I was born outside of L.A., but both of my parents were in the military so we moved a lot. We even lived in Germany for a while. When we returned, I attended UCLA and the University of Southern California."

Both fine schools; I was impressed. We left the house through the back hall, where my mother used to check my father for ticks before he entered the house. Out back, I was amazed to find remnants of my old swing set and the clothesline poles intact.

"It's eerie seeing Anvil Points deserted."

"It may be inhabited again," Walt said. "The jobs are waiting if Project Rulison is the success we think it will be."

I gazed toward the mines and at the mighty shelf of shale above them and quoted my father: "The greatest package of potential energy on the face of the globe."

Walt stared at me. "I know those words. Meg Shaw. Are you Charles Shaw's daughter?"

"You know my father?"

"No, but I've read his writings. He'll be here for the test, right? I'd love to meet him."

"I don't understand. We left twelve years ago. Why would he be here?"

"Why? Because he and Edward Teller are two of the brains behind it. He should see the end results of his work. Teller will be in the viewing area."

Even I had heard of Edward Teller. Some called him the Father of the Hydrogen Bomb. "What does my dad have to do with Edward Teller?"

Walt looked uncomfortable, almost as if he pitied me. "I guess it must have been top secret."

"Secrets. Too many secrets. From our government, our employers, our families, and from each other."

"Calm down, Meg. It's all right."

"It is not all right. My family leaves our home in the dead of the night and never tells me why. A school that doesn't need teachers hires me. And a nuclear bomb is going to be exploded in Colorado on Wednesday, and everyone thinks it's just fine. Where is the press? And please, God, where are the hippies?"

Walt shook his head. "I don't know where to start. I don't understand most of what you just said. But you're right that the government has managed to keep a lid on things. There are lawsuits and injunctions in Washington right now trying to stop the test. I doubt if they'll succeed. The two oil companies paying for it and the politicians have enough power to push it through. There will be some press and even a few of your hippies."

"I still don't understand what my father had to do with anything."

"He designed the whole operation, Meg—in the late forties. It's his baby."

"Then why did we leave so suddenly?" I told Walt about the strange Halloween night in which my life changed.

"I have no idea," Walt said. And he had no idea why the GV School Board wanted me, or why I was having problems reaching my family. But just to be able to talk with someone about it made me feel better. A voice inside said I could be talking to the wrong person. After all, Walt was working for the government and was in favor of the test, but he seemed puzzled, too, and shook his head about Rispa Moore saying Dad should be in jail. "That doesn't make sense. I've always considered your father a hero."

"He's always been mine." The sky was darkening. "We should leave before the storm. The mountains can cloud up pretty fast, and soon you won't see well enough to drive."

Rifle Falls was out, but we drove into Rifle for lunch. Over hamburgers, fries, and Cokes, I asked the question Effie had kept me from asking on Friday. "If the blast is safe, why do we have to move furniture away from the windows and remain outside?"

"A precaution," he assured me. "There's bound to be some tremors. A very slight earthquake, that's all."

That was enough to make a normal person leery, but perhaps a Californian would see it differently.

"Now I have a question. When you overheard the doctor's wife say your father should be in jail, why didn't you let them know you heard? Why didn't you ask why?"

I had asked myself the same thing. "I don't know, exactly. It came as a shock, even though I could tell right away Mrs. Moore didn't approve of me. It didn't seem polite to say anything. After all, they shared their dinner, and Doc Moore was going to drive me to Grand Valley when I didn't know how else to get there."

"Understandable," Walt said. "Maybe you'll have a chance to ask another time."

It rained all the way back to Grand Valley. "That's where Hal Gower works," I said, as we passed the new vanadium mill. "My father had something to do with the old one."

"He certainly did. He designed it, and this one, too."

"Exactly what is vanadium?"

"A mineral. But the chief interest now is the uranium that comes out of its tailings. You've heard of uranium."

"Yes, it's needed to make bombs." I remembered that a few families we knew had become wealthy because of uranium.

The rain was so heavy by the time we reached the Anvil Points Road, we couldn't even see the Book Cliffs. "You were right about us leaving," Walt said.

Yes, I understood the mountains. Even though I'd been away for so long, it all came back. The mountains were a part of me.

Walt said he would be too busy the next day for a drive to Rifle Falls. Was he tired of me? I had treated him to a complex set of emotions. But then he said, "I'll join the Gowers for dinner tomorrow. I could take you up to the site afterward. That is, if you'd like to see it."

Ground Zero—the bombsite—is what he meant. I didn't know if I did, but I wanted to see him. "Thanks," I said.

After supper, Hal whisked Walt away to his study, the boys cleared the table, and I helped Ethel with the dishes. "It's a pleasure to have another gal in the house," Ethel said. "Nothing like a little feminine chatter."

What would be the topic of this chatter? Bombs or the boys' lack of progress in school? I asked her about the phone. "Should I call collect?"

"Just go ahead and call, but wait until late evening when the rates go down. When the phone bill comes, I'll circle the Illinois amount, and we'll settle up then. That okay with you?"

It was perfect. I inquired about laundry and ironing procedures. Then we sat down for yet another cup of coffee, and she asked about my day with Walt.

"We had a good time. He heard about my father before." I told Ethel how surprised Walt had been to find out who I was.

Ethel frowned. "But he already knew that. It bothered me yesterday when he acted like he never knew you lived in Anvil Points. When Walt found out Charles Shaw's daughter would be here, he asked Hal if he could come, too. He wanted to meet you."

"That's strange. Maybe I misunderstood." But I hadn't and needed time to think about what it might mean, so I changed the subject by talking about my life in Anvil Points. Soon Ethel was laughing.

"Your mother said to get out fast if you heard a rattle? I can't imagine! Of course, we always lived in a city where snakes were of a different breed." She sighed. "I'm afraid I've always been protective of my boys—perhaps too much. You've noticed that our Freddy is—different."

"But what a cheerful fellow," I said.

"Doctors say he's a Mongoloid."

"Down Syndrome. I've read about it."

"And then there's Artie." She sighed.

"So talented! I heard him singing last night."

"Oh yes, but the problem is his attitude. He shut down when we moved here. As far as school work goes, he doesn't make any effort."

I told her I'd try to help but not that I was in way over my head. Her boys needed someone with experience—not a brand new teacher.

Later, Freddy invited me to play Monopoly. It was a pleasant way to conclude the evening and to get to know both boys better. Artie seemed to make poor choices deliberately so that Freddy would be more successful. I wondered if he was even aware of doing it.

After everyone went to bed, I called home. The phone rang ten times. Where were they? Almost a whole week had gone by since I talked to Todd. During that time, I had alternated between being scared and angry. Should I call the police? Libby first.

"Libby, it's me."

"Meggy!" She screamed loudly enough to be heard in her whole house and to destroy my hearing. "How are you? I miss you so much!"

"I miss you, too, Libby. How is school going?"

"Just great. My third graders are a delight. I keep seeing you and me at that age." Libby's memory was dim. We hadn't met until fifth grade, but that wasn't important. "How about you, Meg? How's your school?"

"We don't start until Monday, but I'm pretty nervous. I can't talk long. I need a paycheck first so I can pay the phone bill. I'm calling to ask if you know anything about my family. I've tried to reach them, but no one is answering."

"I've been pretty busy. Let's see . . . No, I haven't spoken to any of them since last Sunday night. I drove to your house to see if they'd heard from you and spoke to Todd. I didn't see your parents. I don't think they were home."

My mother's car hadn't been the one Todd heard in the driveway. It was Libby's. Almost a week ago!

Libby chattered on. "Todd said you were fine, but he seemed kind of anxious for me to leave. Do you think he invited his girlfriend over?"

"Teenagers. I guess that's possible."

"Maybe . . . but when I pulled out of the driveway, Todd opened the garage. Your mom's car was there." She giggled. "I'll bet she and your dad were out together, and Todd was going to borrow it."

I had to end this call. "You could be right, but I'm getting worried about all of them. No one is answering the phone, and no one has called to check on me. That isn't like Mom and Dad. Could you go back over there tomorrow?"

"Sure thing. But don't worry. After all, what could happen?"

"Thanks, Libby. I'll call you tomorrow night."

There was another click. Nosy busybodies! I tried home one more time. No answer. "I'll give you until Monday before I call the police," I decided.

Chapter Nine

September 7, Sunday

My own countdown to Wednesday's Project Rulison had begun. Ethel invited me to attend the church service with her. "Nice way to meet people. We like our pastor, although some think he's too modern."

"I'm not much of a church goer, but it would be good to meet more people."

Ethel handed me an envelope. "Almost forgot. Carrie dropped this off yesterday."

Puzzled, I opened it. "Oh good, a schedule of classes for tomorrow. Maybe now I can figure out what I'm going to do."

"You're just learning this?"

I nodded. "Things have been a little disorganized."

Ethel shook her head but didn't say anything.

We walked over to the church, the newest one in town, where Ethel introduced me to some of her friends, whose names didn't register. I smiled, trying to look appreciative when they invited me to join their various committees and causes.

I thought Ethel's minister would be an old man, not the young, blond Viking Pastor Ronald Johanssen turned out to be. Probably more than a few years older than I, but still... I started to compare him with Walt—feature by feature.

Then Pastor Johanssen began his sermon, "Hell Is with Us Now," and I almost forgot his looks. Clearly, the congregation was uncomfortable with the topic: women looked through their purses; men checked their wristwatches and pulled up their socks. One would expect a sermon with that title to be a loud rant about hell and the devil, but the pastor talked quietly about what was about to be unleashed on us—right in Grand Valley. He ended with the most compelling words I'd ever heard in a church service.

"Hell is coming to our valley this Wednesday, and we have allowed greed to convince us it's a good thing. Yes, our community needs more money and work for our people, but will exploding a nuclear bomb achieve this? Do the energy companies represent our interests or their own wallets? Does the government want what's best for Garfield County or more power? Instead of demanding answers to tough questions, we are leaving the work to a few young people who wear their hair in ways we don't approve and sing songs we don't want to hear." I saw Ethel flinch at this.

"Instead of judging them, might we consider that their love of God and the sanctity of this land is greater than ours? I believe we are meddling with affairs best left to God, and I sincerely pray that I am wrong. Please join me now in singing 'Once to Every Man and Nation.'"

I thought the hymn perfect for the occasion and joined in: "Some great cause, some great decision, offering each the bloom or blight. And the choice goes by forever, 'twixt that darkness and that light." But the congregation sang in a lackluster fashion, although they were boisterous in their singing of other songs.

The service ended, and most people exited quickly. Ethel said she had to talk to someone about a recipe, but I wanted to meet the person who had helped me make a decision. His words and choice of music had clarified my thinking. I was the only person to approach him.

"I appreciated your sermon very much."

"I'm glad someone did. You must be the new teacher, Charles Shaw's daughter."

"Meg Shaw. You knew my dad?"

"We were introduced once. I thought him a fine man."

"I don't remember Dad ever going to church." In truth, my parents didn't believe in organized religion. As a child, I attended Sunday School occasionally with friends, but never with my own family.

He chuckled. "No, I wouldn't think so. I met him at a meeting of a . . . a group we both belonged to in Denver."

"Do you remember when that was? We left Colorado suddenly. Some people were surprised."

"Not too surprising the way things were—with the Anvil Points oil shale experiment coming to an end. Your father was smart enough to know when it was time to move on." A few men with solemn faces approached us. "And judging from the reception to my sermon today, it may be time for me to do the same. The Board of Governors—my principals, if you will. Please excuse me."

"I'd like to talk more sometime."

"Better make it soon," he said.

Wishing we could have continued the conversation, I nodded my thanks and left the church. There were so many questions—about his sermon and Project Rulison, but mostly about my father. At least he knew Dad was a good man and didn't think it odd we had left Anvil Points. I hoped Pastor Johanssen wasn't in trouble. The men had looked grim.

Walt and Hal didn't show up for Sunday dinner, although Hal did call. Artie had taken the message. "Dad was all excited. Said it had arrived and was a real beauty."

Freddy began to chant. "The bomb's a beauty, the bomb's a beauty, the bomb's a beauty . . ."

I saw how troubled Ethel and Artie were by Freddy's nonsense and determined to stop him. "Freddy, you must like alliteration." He frowned slightly. "Words that start with the same letter—like Alligators All Around or Big Bad Baboons."

He gave a wide smile. "Big Bad Baboons!"

I had an inspiration. Possibly my only one lately. "Let's make a book of alliterations in school tomorrow."

"A book? Yes! Let's make us one!"

All during the meal, I wondered what Walt was doing and if, thanks to the beautiful bomb, I would see him at all. I recalled what Ethel said about Walt knowing who my father was. Why had he acted as if he didn't? I should ask him, I guessed.

Ethel seemed to be in a bad mood and didn't want help with the dishes. Either the sermon had troubled her, or she was displeased by her husband's non-appearance—or maybe both. The boys decided to work a complicated jigsaw puzzle, so I went to my room and tried to make sense of the teaching schedule. It was doubtful that any beginning teacher had ever been as ill prepared for the first day of school.

Several hours later, I reached a tentative plan for Monday morning. The students would write their personal goals for the year and for their town. And we'd try some alliteration. All kids enjoyed that—I hoped! For social studies, we needed textbooks, once I got them from Carrie's room. Finally, at 3:30, Freddy delivered a message. "Mr. Jeffreys is waiting downstairs for you, Miss Shaw." He frowned. "Can I call you Meg?"

"If it's all right with your parents. At school you should call me Miss Shaw, the way the other kids do. It will be our secret, okay?"

The happy face appeared again. "I love secrets," he confided.

I didn't know how much I could teach Freddy, but I was starting to love him.

Walt was both apologetic and excited. "Hal says we can borrow his car. Sorry I'm so late. I didn't have any way of calling you."

"I had things to do for school tomorrow." He shouldn't know I had been anxious to see him.

"That's right. Tomorrow is a big day for both of us. We'll celebrate. Ethel knows I'm kidnapping you and we won't be back for supper. She seemed relieved. Everything all right?"

"She's just tired; she works hard." I didn't want to get into it. "Let's go. I've never been kidnapped before."

We drove south, across the Colorado River, and up toward the trailhead of Battlement Mesa, not far from Battlement Creek. "Ground Zero," Walt announced when we arrived at a totally flat surface. He had been stopped several times to show his identification badge to armed security guards. The guns made sense, although it was unlikely anyone would steal a bomb. There were a number of vehicles, which according to the signs on them, were the property of Austral Oil and CER Geonuclear, the two companies paying for the test, and a long flatbed covered with a tarp. I could guess what was under it.

"Is this all federal land?" I looked out at endless acres.

Walt hesitated. "Well, not this exact location. I'm not too happy about the way some of my colleagues have handled things."

"The land belongs to someone, and the Atomic Energy Commission just took it." I paraphrased Sadie Eicher's angry words outside the town hall.

"Not quite that bad. We are paying for it."

"A lot?" Well, he wasn't sure.

Later, I learned that much of the land had been taken from private citizens, such as Sadie, and that the site for Ground Zero, itself, was part of 292 acres owned by a 73-year-old potato farmer. Officials from the AEC got him drunk and promised him two-hundred dollars a month for the rest of his life if he lent his land for the project. His son protested because he was afraid the test would pollute his creek, causing the land to become worthless, but the farmer was gullible and signed the agreement. He never received a dime of the promised money, and his son's prophecy about the water proved accurate.

"Look, Meg. They're uncovering it now." A team of men moved into place and carefully removed the tarp. Walt whistled. "What a beauty!"

"Beautiful bomb," I whispered. This was a science fiction movie, totally unreal. It looked like a child's creation—maybe something made from taped-together toilet paper tubes. One half was painted silver and the other, a black, red, and yellow diamond pattern. It resembled a pencil—Skinny Boy—approximately nine inches in diameter. I remembered the size of the well it would occupy. "Eight thousand four hundred-thirty feet deep and fifteen inches wide."

"Good memory." Walt beamed, not sensing my alarm. He could have been Freddy with a new toy. "They'll drop her tomorrow. Then we wait for word from Washington that the lawsuit has been dismissed." He seemed certain it would be.

"It's not a her. I've christened him Skinny Boy, and I think he's scary."

"Powerful," he agreed, misunderstanding me, "and the start of more tests to stimulate gas production—right here in Colorado. A positive will come from something the world considers a negative."

I shuddered. "More than twice as powerful as Hiroshima."

"But perfectly safe, Meg."

I prayed he was right.

Time to think about supper. I had no appetite, but Walt was hungry. Sunday night in Grand Valley—nothing would be open. "The Old Midland in Rifle," Walt suggested.

"Fine." I didn't care where we went. Home to Des Plaines would have sounded good. "Not late, though. I start teaching tomorrow."

"And I have to be at Ground Zero early. An exciting day for us both."

He turned on the car radio, and I was pleased to have the Edwin Hawkins Singers distract me, although "Oh Happy Day" didn't reflect my mood. He asked if I had managed to call home. "No one answered. I'll try again tonight." I didn't feel like talking about it or anything else. I should ask about Ethel's comment about his wanting to meet me because of my father, but I decided to wait.

The Old Midland's restaurant boasted a large crowd for a Sunday night, but they managed to seat us. It would be hard to hear each other, but I still wasn't in the mood for conversation. We ordered steaks and a bottle of wine. "To celebrate," he said.

The Moores were eating several tables away. Rispa saw us and stuck her head in a menu. Doc Moore must have noticed, for he looked in our direction and waved.

"My former doctor and his wife," I said.

"Go ask what they meant about your father."

"Not here." Our order came, and I forgot I wasn't hungry.

We were just finishing when Doc Moore and Rispa approached our table. They seemed surprised when they learned Walt's identity.

"We're praying that Rulison project of yours is successful. For all of our sakes," Doc said.

"Especially for Clyde Hardy's," Rispa added.

"Who?" The name was unfamiliar.

"The farmer whose land you stole."

"Come now," Walt said. "We paid for it."

"Precious little. And he hasn't seen any money yet."

Doc Moore placed his hand on his wife's shoulder. "We're worried about Clyde's health. He has a heart condition and that farm means everything to him. If your test pollutes the creek or ruins the land, it will kill him."

"That won't happen," Walt said.

"We'll hold you to that promise, Mr. Jeffreys." Rispa stormed out of the restaurant.

Doc Moore smiled an apology. He told Walt it was a pleasure meeting him and wished me luck in school. "I'll come see you real soon, Meg."

I thought Walt seemed troubled. "You can't blame people for questioning this."

"I know. I just wish I could make them understand how their lives will improve. Well, they'll have to see for themselves."

We rode silently back to Grand Valley. Before we went into the house, still in the car, Walt leaned over and kissed me. Just a simple, beginning kiss. "It will be okay, Meg."

"Be careful of those promises, Walt. Good night." I hurried into the house.

Inside, Walt disappeared into Hal's study. Ethel and the boys had gone upstairs already. In the kitchen, supper dishes, although clean, were still stacked in the drainer. I put them away, packed a lunch, and tried not to think about the following day. I was a kid again, not wanting Monday to come—not wanting to go to school.

I called Libby, but there was no answer. Now what? Would my first day of teaching include calling the police?

Chapter Ten

September 8, Monday

INSPIRATION CAME ON MY WAY to breakfast. Ethel was absent, but I could hear the washing machine whirring in the back hall. I helped myself to fruit and cereal before joining the boys. "Artie," I said, "I want you to bring your guitar to school."

"No way." But he was curious. "Why?"

"An idea I have for teaching literature, writing, all of it—in one fell swoop."

"With my guitar?"

"And you. The students would be songwriters, with you setting their words to music. I'll bet you've composed songs before. In fact, didn't you write that song about the bomb being perfectly safe? The one I said sounded like Tom Lehrer?"

"Well, yeah, but that took me a long time. Their stuff would be lame."

"Some of it—at first anyway. But isn't that true of all songwriters when they start out?"

Artie was interested but determined not to show it. "What about Freddy? How does he fit in?"

"Are you kidding? He's a natural. Do you remember alliteration, Freddy?"

Freddy came through. "Big bad baboon," he said.

Artie couldn't suppress a grin. "Don't forget Beautiful Bomb," he added.

"Big Bad Beautiful Bomb. Don't you think you could come up with some music for Freddy's alliteration poems?"

"I could, but why should I?"

"To help me, for one thing. Look, Artie, I need to succeed at this job. All the teaching positions back home have been filled. If I have to go home because I've failed, I'll have nothing."

He snorted. "Why should you fail? You don't need me."

"I think I do. My plans for today are boring. I need something that will excite the kids. So far, I haven't had much help from anyone. They don't seem to want me here."

Silence, until Freddy said, "We want you, Meg."

Artie nodded. "Okay, I'll lug the guitar to school, but what should I do with it when I get there?"

"Leave it in my classroom—Room 10. Maybe you should put it in the cloakroom where it will be safe—less noticeable."

Artie could grasp paranoia. "Good idea." He took his dishes to the sink. "Better hustle, Freddy."

Artie didn't know it, but he was about to become my teaching assistant. "Do you have any songbooks I can borrow? I'll type out a few songs so the kids can see that some of them started out as poems."

"I have a Pete Seeger one. I'll get it for you."

"Perfect," I said. I'd teach using folk music and protest songs.

I stuck my head into the laundry area to say goodbye to Ethel and noticed a blackboard hanging near the dryer. Chalk. I forgot to buy some in Rifle. "Ethel, do you have a piece of chalk I could take to school?"

"Sure, but don't you have any in your classroom?"

"I couldn't find any." I left it at that. No need to upset her. She seemed in better spirits today. "Wish me luck," I said.

"You just work my boys hard."

"I'll try."

In Room 10, after making sure the guitar was safely in the cloakroom, I set up my typewriter and inserted one of the blank dittoes mailed from home. Before I typed anything, I checked that the ditto machine was working.

Effie Winn was hunched over her coffee in the staffroom. She looked up at me and scowled.

"Good morning, Effie. You must not have a homeroom, either."

"Why did the Gower boy bring a guitar to school? He took it to your room. You do remember that I'm the music teacher?"

"Of course I do. I can't teach music. Artie is going to use his guitar to help me with a poetry writing lesson."

"That's odd," she said. "I don't think that's in your curriculum."

I had tried to be polite, but her rudeness and hostility were an especially cruel way to start the day. "Actually, the curriculum guide is so dated it's useless, and my classroom is practically bare. I'm depending on my wits and imagination just to be able to handle things."

She seemed flustered—anxious to get away from me. "Well, if you need anything, just ask."

"I do need to know if the ditto machine is working," I said.

"I couldn't say." And she was gone.

What just happened? She had been pleasant enough before. I checked out the machine by cranking out a copy from a ditto master left behind. Seemed fine. I finished making my song copies at exactly 9:00, the same time Carrie came into the staff room. "Oh, good, Carrie. I was hoping to see you."

"Hi. You all set?"

Her words were friendly, but I sensed a new reserve. "For this morning, I think, but I need textbooks, and they're all in your room."

"Oh, sure. We'll take care of that real soon."

"During lunch," I said. "I need them this afternoon."

"Well, if I have time."

"Carrie, what going on? I thought you wanted to be friends. You've obviously changed your mind. Why?"

She looked glum—worried. I waited. "Your bulletin boards," she said finally.

"My bulletin boards? What do they have to do with anything?"

"They're wonderful. I thought—that is, it looked like you were trying to show us up—to prove you're better than we are."

"Carrie!" I was going to let her have it. "I don't have the posters or charts the rest of you do. I was given no supplies and no help. It's been ridiculous. I had to ask Ethel Gower for a piece of chalk because Mrs. Arnold refused to give me one. I used my own money to buy supplies at the ten-cent store for the hand-made posters I made in a tiny cheap room at the Rifle Y, where I stayed during orientation because no one bothered to tell me about it until the last moment."

"I'm sorry," she said. "I guess I wasn't thinking."

I shook my head. "No, there's got to be more to it than that."

"All right. I thought we were going to be friends, too, but then Ruth and now Effie started talking to me."

"About what?"

"Well, they said it was strange the board hired a new teacher when we don't need one, and they said you were after my job."

I couldn't believe this was happening. "Carrie, they are wrong. Yes, something strange is going on, but I'm sure it has nothing to do with you. After the Rifle school rejected me, I received a letter from the GV Board asking me to apply. Foolishly, I never examined how strange that was.

I've never heard of a school asking an unknown first-year teacher to apply, have you?"

She shook her head.

"There's been one weird thing after another since I arrived, and right now, I wish I could go home. No one wants me here, and I miss my family. Please believe me. I would quit before putting your job in jeopardy.

"I'm sorry, Meg."

"Apology accepted. Can we start again?"

She looked sheepish but smiled and nodded. "Have lunch in my room today, and we can get some of the kids to haul the books into your room. Would that be soon enough?"

"Yes, thanks." We would get along now, but I was not as eager for her friendship as I had been. She was petty, and it looked as if the other teachers were, too. Other than Artie, Freddy (and possibly Walt while he was still around), I didn't have any friends in Grand Valley. But I clearly had enemies.

When lunchtime came, I was sorry about agreeing to eat with Carrie. I wanted to be alone—to gloat, to re-live my morning. Thanks to Artie, my lesson was a great hit and so much fun. He was reluctant, at first, but relaxed as soon as the guitar came out of its case and he started to sing. I had hopes the students would soon see Artie as a leader—their own "rock star."

In addition to Artie and Freddy, my class consisted of Trudy, Elena, and Karen—age eleven, Barbara, Betty, and Joyce—twelve, Reggie—thirteen, and Mike—ten. Artie and Betty seemed the most mature and Mike, the smartest. Reggie had severe learning problems.

After we listened to Artie, I put students into groups to work on creating their own songs. I could tell Artie was not pleased Freddy and Reggie were together. I had him work with Mike, the youngest. Occasionally, I saw Artie peeking at his brother. Finally, he turned to me and nodded. He understood. Freddy was enjoying his rare role as leader, and both he and Reggie were taking themselves seriously, finding rhyming words for lyrics.

As lunchtime approached, I asked them to write out their songs as neatly as possible. I would type them so we could work on them again the next day.

"Tomorrow?" Betty said. "Can't we work on them this afternoon?"

"This afternoon we'll have social studies."

"Social Studies!" They all groaned.

Surprisingly, Artie came to my rescue. "Give her a chance. We just had reading, writing, spelling, and handwriting, but you didn't seem to mind."

"We did?" Reggie looked to Freddy for confirmation. Freddy, of course, always agreed with Artie and nodded happily.

"Maybe tonight, Artie will look over your songs and see if you need to make any changes before he can set them to music," I suggested. He agreed.

During lunch, Carrie and I didn't have much to say to each other. She complained about the amount of papers she had to grade that evening. I thought about the five songs I was looking forward to reading and typing, so said nothing. I asked her why Mike was in my class. "He's only ten," I said.

"But he's very bright, and he knows it. His parents also know it and will be certain to tell you you're not challenging him enough."

So that was the reason. Carrie wasn't up to the challenge. "Well, I'm pleased to have him," I said.

She changed the subject. "My parents saw you with one of the Project Rulison men last night at the Old Midland in Rifle. You're a fast worker. Are you dating?"

If her parents were like Carrie, then everyone in Grand Valley knew. "I hardly know him," I said. "He's a friend of Hal Gower's. Hal asked me to show him around. We bumped into my old doctor and his wife in the restaurant. Doc Moore. I was glad to see him again."

Hopefully, that would settle the matter. But were Walt and I dating? Hardly. But we were doing something. I wondered if it had been planted yet, or whatever it's called when a bomb is buried deep in the earth. I did want to see Walt again, and then again, I didn't.

The rest of the day was awkward and dull. We opened the Social Studies texts and began plodding through Colonial America. The same students who had been so alive that morning turned into spiritless robots, although Mike and Betty gave me puzzled glances, as if to accuse me of betrayal. Finally, I gave up. "You're right. This is boring. We must find ways to make what we need to learn more interesting. Pass the books to the front, and stack them in the closet." They rushed to obey. We returned to working on our songs for the remaining time.

During a break, I typed up their efforts and gave copies to Artie when he picked up his guitar after school. "Shall I bring it again tomorrow?" I nodded. Then I received my bouquet for the day. "It was cool, Meg," he said.

"Social Studies wasn't."

"No, but at least you stopped it. Most teachers wouldn't have."

Feeling discouraged but not defeated, I decided to visit Loreen. I hadn't seen her since that Halloween night so many years ago but was certain she would remember me.

The address couldn't be right. I stared at a once-gray house with paint hanging off its sides in great peels. Shutters hung loose; shingles were missing from the roof. Carefully, I climbed the wooden stairs of a rickety front porch—no railing, no doorbell. Tentatively, I knocked on the door.

A young child was wailing and an adult scolded. Finally, a woman opened the door. This couldn't be Loreen. Loreen was pretty. This woman was gaunt, undernourished, with oily, unstyled hair drooping along her shoulders. She wore the kind of housedress our mothers wore in the early 50s. "Loreen?"

"So it's you. Heard you were back. Surprised you had the nerve."

"I don't understand."

"Sure you do. You've come back with all your money to lord it over us. I suppose your father is lurking around, too." Another wail came from inside. "Oh, go away. I don't have time to talk to you. Some of us have real jobs." She slammed the door in my face.

Shaken, I tried to accept what had just happened—that the pretty little girl who had been my best friend from the first day of first grade until we were ten was now a sour, unhappy woman. Even then, I knew her home life was more difficult than mine, and I guessed it had continued to be. But I hadn't caused her problems.

Back at the Gowers', Ethel had returned to her foul mood. "They're not coming for supper again," she said, banging pots and pans. "Hal and Walt are 'too tied up with the project.' That's all they can think about."

I thought the project was probably all any of us should be thinking about, but I tried to soothe her. "Day after tomorrow it will be over."

"But meanwhile, there's supper."

"Let's keep it simple," I said, although I was hungry enough for a 5-course meal. "I'll bet there are plenty of leftovers we can heat up."

We worked together, foraging for possibilities in the refrigerator. I kept up a stream of chatter, and she seemed to relax. "And how did my boys do?"

"Just fine—at least in my classes. I don't know about arithmetic and science, of course. Do you know if they have homework?"

"Freddy said he had arithmetic, but it was too hard for him. Artie doesn't do homework."

I offered to help Freddy and borrowed some buttons for counters. "It might help if he can visualize the numbers," I explained.

Freddy was glued to a television cartoon. I sat on the floor and started to lay out buttons on the coffee table. It proved to be a greater novelty, and he soon joined me. "What are you doing, Meg?"

"Turn off the TV, and I'll show you." He rushed to obey. "Now we'll need your homework and a pencil."

Freddy frowned. "Artie says it's stupid."

"Well, I'm the teacher—not Artie—and I say it isn't stupid. And Freddy, you aren't stupid either."

Freddy flushed with pleasure. The buttons would be helpful in solving the basic addition problems. "Four buttons plus four buttons. Count them, Freddy."

"I count eight buttons!" And he wrote the answer carefully on his paper. After ten problems, the homework was complete. Sometimes, he wrote the numbers backward and had to erase and try again, but he was determined to see it through. Triumphantly, he carried the paper into the kitchen to show his mother, and then put it carefully into his notebook. "Mom says it's time for supper. I'll get Artie."

I wondered if Artie had tried to accomplish anything with the songs, but it would be a mistake to ask him while we were eating. I waited to see if he brought up the subject. Naturally, he didn't.

Later, I could hear Artie playing his guitar and singing.

Oh, there'll be gas for Grand Valley
And nearby Rifle, too.
But the folks out on the mesa
Are likely to get screwed.

Pete Seeger and Tom Lehrer had some serious competition.

"Let's sing my Big Bad Boom song, Artie."

I longed to join them but held back. Finally, all was quiet in Artie's room. Soon I heard Ethel go into her bedroom. It was time for me to return to the kitchen to use the telephone.

First, I tried home, not expecting an answer. I allowed twenty rings before calling Libby. "Hello." She yawned.

"It's me. You sound tired."

"Busy day, and it's past 11:00 here."

Right—the time difference. "Sorry, I forgot. What did you find out?"

"Nothing good, Meggy. I called Maine East. Todd wasn't in school, and no one called him in sick."

"Did you go over to our house?"

"Yesterday. No time today. But no one was there. I peeked into the garage. Both cars are gone now."

"I'm scared, Libby. I guess I'll have to call the police."

"They'll make you file a missing persons report, and it's probably just nothing. Is there a spare key somewhere? I could go inside and poke around tomorrow."

After telling her where to find the key, I sat frozen, not really listening as she told me all of her fellow teachers were going to defy the dress code and wear pantsuits to school the next day. "I've got the cutest one, black polyester with white trim . . ."

If only I were back home, thinking what I wore to school was important. This whole Colorado adventure had been a mistake. I should quit and return to where old friends wouldn't betray me, and no one would set off a nuclear bomb and think it was a good idea. Libby finally said goodbye. The tears that had been stored up for over a week began to fall—just as Walt came into the kitchen.

"Hey, what's this about? Tears? Was it such a bad day?"

I sobbed onto his shoulder. "Oh, Walt, it was like four days. Some of it was fine, but most of it was awful."

Chapter Eleven

September 9, Tuesday

ANOTHER DIFFICULT DAY AT SCHOOL. The songwriting was going well, but we couldn't do that indefinitely. Making Social Studies interesting was still a challenge. And it was becoming impossible to think of anything but the bomb—and my family. I remembered that Pastor Johanssen had known my father, so I called during lunchtime to make an appointment. As soon as school ended, I hurried over to the church and found Pastor Johanssen waiting for me in his office.

"How may I help you, Miss Shaw?"

There was something about him that told me formalities weren't necessary. "Please call me Meg," I said. "It's a little hard to explain. I would like to know more about my father—about how you met him. On Sunday, you said he was a fine man. I'm not sure everyone shares your opinion." I gave him some background on what I'd experienced since arriving—especially Rispa Moore's words and Loreen's reaction to seeing me, and the circumstances of my obtaining the GV teaching job. "It's clear they don't need another teacher. But the main problem is my family—they're missing!" And I told him about both Libby's and my inability to contact them over several days. "They've vanished, and I'm frightened."

"Phew!" Pastor Johanssen settled back in his chair. "You've thrown out a lot of different issues. Let's start with what I know. I was introduced to Charles Shaw at a meeting I attended in Denver when I was a divinity student. It must have been about twelve years ago."

"That's how long it's been since we left Anvil Points. What kind of meeting was it?"

He hesitated. "Normally, I don't talk about it because so many people wouldn't understand." He sighed. "May we keep this conversation between us?"

"Of course."

"It was a meeting of scientists, engineers, and religious people—ministers, priests, rabbis—who were concerned with the notion of using nuclear devices for peaceful purposes. We weren't against the idea *per se;* we were worried that not enough thinking or planning had taken place to determine the results of the proposed testing. I'm still uncertain."

"And it will happen tomorrow. I'm confused, though. This isn't the first test in," I winced, "Operation Plowshare." He smiled at my discomfort with the term. "The other tests were successful."

"Were they? I wonder. The results are all classified. I have never read or been told anything I thought was factual."

"Why you do feel you can't talk about your group in Denver, Pastor Johanssen?"

"Because it doesn't exist anymore, and those who were there don't want their connection with it known. The government investigated and decided it was a Communist front. This was several years after the Army-McCarthy hearings, thank the Lord, or things could have been terribly difficult for many more innocent, concerned citizens."

"But my dad? Why was he at the meeting? A friend of mine who works for the AEC considers my father a hero because he designed some of the things that are being used in the tests."

"Walt Jeffreys." Pastor Johanssen nodded. "I heard you were seeing him." At my expression, he chuckled. "Very hard to keep a secret in Grand Valley."

"He's a friend of the Gowers," I said. "I've only known him for a few days. But my dad . . ."

"Yes. Your father is a brilliant man, whose calculations led him to believe the resulting radioactivity was enough reason for the whole operation to be shut down—perhaps forever. He gave a stirring address that moved all of us—especially those of us entering the ministry."

"But my father is an atheist."

"Chet Shaw is a humanist. His religion is earth-centered and about the goodness of people. I wouldn't dream of objecting to that."

"He's a wonderful father. I just wish I knew where he was. Do you think I should contact the police?"

He nodded. "If your friend can't find anything, I'm afraid you'll have to."

I had taken up enough of his time. He asked me to keep him informed and added that I should call him Ron. This seemed a little strange, but I'd never known a minister so young before. Certainly he couldn't be *much* older than I—I hoped. He was easy to talk to, and the prospect of having a real friend felt good. Foolishly, I thought he might be interested in me. That felt good, too.

Hal and Walt had come home early and would join us for supper. Everyone was in the kitchen, trying to help Ethel with preparations, much to her dismay. The large kitchen suddenly seemed quite small—the men as giddy as children as they chatted excitedly about the next day. I decided not to add to the confusion and went upstairs to freshen up.

Freddy followed me. "Can we play the button game again after supper? Mrs. Arnold liked my homework."

I wanted to spend time with Walt, but Freddy needed me. "Do you have homework again tonight, Freddy?"

He shuddered. "It's subtraction. Much harder."

"Then of course we'll use the buttons." I wondered if Ruth Arnold knew of my interference.

At supper, when I was able to get a word in, I asked Walt about the other tests. "Have you been to all of them?"

"Hardly. I was too young. The first was in New Mexico in 1961, but it yielded only three kilotons of energy." At my puzzled look, he added, "a lot of TNT."

"Boom!" Freddy said helpfully.

"New Mexico. Most have been in Nevada, haven't they?" Ethel asked.

"That's right. I was involved in—let's see—four tests there, and one in New Mexico. This is the first in Colorado, and if all goes well, there will be more to come."

"Just imagine," Hal put down his fork, joining the conversation, "the explosions will break the natural gas away from the rocks, creating a cavern of gas, just ready for the pumping. Grand Valley will become a center of production."

"And our engineers believe," Walt continued, "that the caverns will join underground, forming a gigantic storage facility for this gas."

"Right near Battlement Creek and the Colorado River." I exchanged looks with Artie, who looked as displeased as I felt. He knew better than to say anything in front of his father, though. And judging from Hal and Walt's reaction, it would have been better for me to remain quiet.

"As I've told you, over and over, Meg, it's perfectly safe." It wasn't my imagination. Walt was irritated with me.

"I saw Clyde's son, Lee, at the post office today." Ethel had decided to enter the fray. "He was very upset. Claimed the only reason Clyde signed his land away was because the government got him drunk."

Hal snorted. "Now, Ethel, you know it doesn't take much to get that old man drunk."

"And the land is still his," Walt added, "except right around Ground Zero."

I didn't say what I was thinking—that way more than that small area would be needed when the time ever came to start pumping. I remembered the sheepish way Walt had reacted when I asked him about the farmer. It was apparent Walt was not comfortable with the way things had been handled.

But Ethel was not quite ready to give up. "The only thing that land has going for it is the clean water nearby," she said. "Without it, the land will be worthless. Nothing will grow, not even potatoes."

"The water will be fine," Walt snapped.

We finished our supper in silence. It was just as well I had a date with Freddy. I no longer wanted to be alone with Walt, although it appeared that wasn't an option. Hal said he and Walt were going out "for a spell."

"Probably for a pre-celebratory drink," Ethel said. Artie fled upstairs, and Freddy waited for me in the living room. I told Ethel I'd do the dishes, so she handed me the dishtowel. "I can't wait for the whole damn thing to be over," she said, and left me alone with the dishes—and the telephone. Quickly, I called Libby.

"Libby, did you find anything?"

"Yes, but not much. No notes, but next to the telephone I found a slip of paper with a long distance number on it." She hesitated.

"And?"

"I wasn't sure it was the right thing to do, but I dialed it from your house."

"Good. What happened?"

"It was the number of a hotel in Washington, D.C. The Manger Hay-Adams. I gave your parents' name, and they started to connect me, but I hung up."

"Why did you do that?"

"Because I didn't know what to say. At least you know where they are now."

What could I say? None of this was her fault. I asked for the phone number.

"Oh, it's still at your house. I didn't think . . ."

I heard the familiar click of someone else on the line. "That's okay, Libby. You're right. Now I know where they are. Thank you for everything."

Washington, D.C. It made sense in a way. Pastor Johanssen had told me Dad was against the tests. Probably he was testifying at the hearings. Todd must be with them. That click bothered me, but I had to know. "Operator, please give me the phone number of the Manger Hay-Adams Hotel."

Soon—"I'm sorry, your party must not be in the room. Please call back." Well, I would, but not that night.

Chapter Twelve

Wednesday, September 10

THE DAY OF THE BOMB—Project Rulison. I awoke to sounds of confusion and the smell of bacon and wondered if it were going to be a very long or very short day.

Downstairs, Hal, Walt, and the boys were opening windows and moving furniture away from them. "Do I need to do anything upstairs?"

"Good morning, Meg." Walt greeted me with an enthusiastic hug, not seeming to mind if anyone noticed. "Unless you've got something in front of the windows, you should be okay. Just make sure to open them and don't leave any loose papers around." I never saw anyone so excited unless under the age of five and having a birthday party.

"This is it," Hal said. "The big day we've waited for."

I let them carry on and joined Ethel in the kitchen. "Well, they're certainly happy."

"You'd think the circus had come to town. And the traffic—since about five this morning. Up and down First Street—a regular parade of cars."

"Every circus needs a parade," I said. "I wonder if I'll get anything done at school."

"Doubtful. I'm not sure why they're even bothering with it today."

I tried calling D.C. again. My parents weren't picking up the receiver in their room, but at least I knew where they were, and I felt sure Todd must be there, too. I left a message for them to call the Gowers'. Perhaps I could replace being scared with being angry. What excuse could they possibly have for not calling?

Carrie came to walk to school with me. I wanted to be alone with my thoughts but couldn't refuse her new attempt at friendship. The streets were crowded with strange cars and strange people. "Who are they? Reporters?"

"Some, and probably a few protestors. They're trying to get in before all the roads are barricaded."

"Barricaded?"

Carrie explained. "Starting at about ten-thirty, no cars will be able to get in or out until the blast is over. Only people who were invited will be at the viewing area."

Made sense, I guessed. Safety, alone, dictated that the numbers be kept small. "Who's on the invitation list?"

"The governor, mayors of Rifle, Grand Junction, and Glenwood Springs—important people like that. And that science fellow. I forget his name."

"Edward Teller, the father of the hydrogen bomb," I said.

"That's right. You've brought your lunch, Meg. Why?"

I laughed. "To eat, of course."

"Didn't you hear? There's going to be a picnic in the park—for everyone. The Women's Alliance from the Methodist Church is providing it. Remember, everyone has to stay out-of-doors."

"I didn't know about the picnic." It was to be a circus, Memorial Day, and the 4th of July, all rolled into one. Complete with fireworks.

At school, we learned two things, both from Effie Winn, who greeted us at the door. "No homeroom or first period classes. We'll have an assembly, and I'm in charge. Mr. Owens left the whole thing up to me. Oh, and Ruth called in sick. Mr. Owens isn't getting a sub, either."

"Too bad she's sick," Carrie said. "She'll miss all the excitement. But there won't be many kids. A lot of the parents will keep them home. Let's just divide up whoever comes."

Two students noticeably absent were Artie and Freddy. No one had said anything at breakfast about their staying home, but something could have changed. The morning passed slowly with meaningless activity. Effie led us in all the patriotic songs she could think of—"You're a Grand Old Flag," "America the Beautiful," among others. I thought Artie's song or even Freddy's "Big Bad Beautiful Bomb" would have been more appropriate, except for the part about "the bombs bursting in air" in "The Star Spangled Banner." After Effie's sing-along, we went from room to room, moving furniture away from the open windows. Finally, noon came, and everyone left the building and headed for the park.

Somehow, the carnival atmosphere seemed wrong, so I walked past the park. A few people, definitely not hippies, were holding protest signs. Wandering aimlessly near the outskirts of town, I recognized two people far ahead, starting up a rocky hill that would lead to a bridge crossing the Colorado River. My AWOL students, Artie and Freddy! Where were they going? Only one possible answer. I raced to catch up with them.

"Okay, boys, what are you up to?"

Freddy's face lit up. "Meg, are you coming with us?"

But Artie scowled. "What are you doing here?"

"Answer my question first." He shook his head. "Very well. Freddy, where are you and Artie going?"

"We're going to be bare witnesses. Only I think we should keep our clothes on."

This outlandish remark broke the ice. Neither Artie nor I could suppress a grin. He tried to explain. "We're going to bear witness to history, Freddy. Just like Miss Shaw said we should do. That means we're going to see it for ourselves."

Oh, dear, that is what I said. "But I didn't mean you should actually go to where the bomb is. I meant we would all bear witness simply by being present today in Grand Valley."

"Not good enough. I don't trust them to tell us the truth."

I didn't either, but I wasn't going to admit it.

"Come with us, Meg. Our lunch is better than yours. We'll share."

I smiled at Freddy. "What have you two been doing all morning when you should have been in school?"

"Did we miss a lot?" Artie asked sarcastically. I shook my head. He hadn't missed a thing.

"Please, just answer the question."

"We were getting supplies together and planning our route. We had to wait until the house was clear before we could go back and get what we needed."

His backpack looked as if it might contain a week's worth of supplies. For all his rough ways, Artie was still a kid, and this must seem like a great adventure. "I don't know how close you'll be able to get, but I'll go with you." I mentioned the roadblocks and told them about the guards with rifles I'd seen on Sunday.

"Well, seeing as how you're here, you might as well come along. It's not going to be an easy hike, though."

It wasn't, and I was in no shape for the trek over the rocky slopes, nor was I dressed for adventure. Artie couldn't help me because Freddy needed an extra hand even more than I did. We needed to stay away from the roads, so we wouldn't be noticed. As soon as we crossed the Colorado River on the narrow, swaying footbridge, we were faced with steep paths overgrown with weeds. In the distance, we could see both the blockades and guards. Several years or miles later, we finally saw the viewing area. A large circus tent, honoring the theme of the day, had been erected for groups gathered under and near it. I thought I saw Hal Gower and, yes, Doc Moore and his wife.

Then, my eyes zeroed in on a distant boulder. Two men were standing next to it, talking, and I recognized one of them. My father!

"Come on, Meg." Artie pulled me away. "Do you want to be seen? We need to get closer to the bomb."

I stumbled the rest of the way. My legs were tired, shoes, stockings, and best school skirt ruined, but that didn't trouble me as much as my thoughts. Yes, the person I saw was far away, but it was my father—I was certain. And what was my father doing here when he was registered at the Hay-Adams in D.C.?

We finally climbed the hill, overlooking the flat land of Ground Zero. The rigs had been moved away, although a few of the mayor's trucks were there. We were the only people.

"This isn't Ground Zero," Freddy said. "Who will push the button for the boom?"

"This is the place." Ruth Arnold appeared suddenly from behind an overgrowth of sagebrush. "The bomb is underground now, Freddy. Someone will push the button remotely from far away."

"Mrs. Arnold, you're here, too?"

"It appears she is, Freddy," I said, "and no longer sick."

"I am sick. Sick at heart about what's going to happen today. But this is dangerous. Why are you here?"

"We're the bare witnesses, but Meg says we can keep our clothes on."

Ruth smiled at Freddy, and I could tell she cared about him. Then she turned on me. "Considering who your father is and your unofficial boyfriend, I would have expected you to be in the viewing area."

"I wasn't invited," I said. "Besides, other than needing to chaperone these two characters, I belong here."

She sneered. "And why is that?"

It was time—finally—to take a stand. "Because I think exploding a nuclear bomb is the worst thing that's ever happened to Colorado. I'm afraid for the state and my country and friends. And like Freddy said, I'm going to be a bare witness, too."

Chapter Thirteen

For now, Ruth decided to give me the benefit of the doubt. The four of us sat on the ground and waited. We didn't know when zero hour would be, but it couldn't be much longer.

"I'm thinking of something," Freddy said.

"Oh good—a guessing game. Should we guess what color it is?" I asked.

"No," he said, impatiently for him. "I'm thinking there are big rocks in back of us and big rocks in front of us. Won't the boom make the rocks come down and smash us to bits?"

We looked at each other in horror. "You're absolutely right, Freddy," Ruth said. "Come on—there's no one here to see us. We need to be on level ground away from the boulders."

Proudly, Artie patted Freddy on the shoulder. "My brother is plenty smart in his own way." Freddy just beamed.

We scrambled down the hill and found a place to hide behind some sagebrush, where we would remain somewhat hidden but far enough away from the treacherous rocks. Artie amused Freddy by taking photos of the area. They didn't seem to be paying attention to Ruth and me.

"I still have a lot of doubts and questions about your father," she said.

I sighed. "So do I, Ruth. But one thing you need to know—I am not my father."

"I can see that."

Silently, we watched the boys for a few minutes. "Why are you here? Why did you come to Grand Valley?"

"To teach, I thought." I told her about the letter that had come to the placement office.

"You didn't think that strange?"

"I didn't think at all. It was disappointing when they turned me down in Rifle, and then the letter happened. Well, I wanted to come back to Colorado. Now, it seems a giant mistake. No one wants me here."

"You're wrong about that," Ruth said. "Someone does. Someone set the whole thing up."

We might have talked more, but the boys joined us. "This is fun," Freddy said. "We have the whole place to ourselves. We'll see Project Boom better than anyone."

Ruth, Artie, and I looked at each other, coming to the same conclusion at once. "If it's so safe," Artie said slowly, "then where is everyone? Why isn't the safe viewing stand right here?"

"Oh, for goodness sake! Let's get out of here!" Ruth ordered.

The four of us ran, Artie helping Freddy, who was unable to move as quickly. "The bushes over there," Artie shouted.

Then we heard it. Not the explosion, although we thought so at first because that's what we were expecting, but the hump-thump wop-wop of a helicopter coming closer. It landed near us, although I didn't think we'd been seen.

"Copter!" Freddy raced toward the helicopter.

"Freddy, no!" Artie thrust the camera toward me and ran after his brother. Mindlessly, I began taking pictures.

A shot rang out of nowhere, and Freddy collapsed on the ground. Artie screamed in anger and terror. "You shot Freddy?"

I started to leave our cover, but Ruth grabbed me. "No," she warned. "You'll get shot, too."

The helicopter door opened, and a man jumped out, holding his hand up, yelling as if to indicate the rifleman should hold his fire. Because of the spinning blades, we couldn't hear anything. Artie and the man helped Freddy to his feet. "We have to go to them," I said—just as the explosion began. Artie and Freddy were pushed inside, as the helicopter lifted off. It veered and shook but managed to fly away. Ruth and I lay on the ground, clinging to each other.

Nightmares about those moments and the next stayed with me for years. After the initial explosion, a second one, more like a rumble, came along that lifted us a full eight inches into the air. Some of the noise came from underground, but the loudest sounds were from crashing boulders. Huge plumes of dust prevented us from seeing clearly, but ripples of earth, like waves of water, moved toward us, and we gagged, choking on the dust. We couldn't leave, but we couldn't stay, either.

Summoning all our strength in spite of the continuing aftershocks, Ruth and I stumbled our way toward town. This time, we took the roads; it no longer mattered if we were seen. I couldn't stop sobbing. How badly was Freddy hurt, and where were the boys taken? We desperately needed help!

We separated when we reached Grand Valley. My task was to find Ethel. Ruth said she'd tell Pastor Johanssen and get help alerting everyone. Before we parted, Ruth gave me a fierce hug. "Tell as many people as you can, Meg. We'll find each other later."

Chapter Fourteen

Grand Valley had become a rubble of rocks, tumbleweeds, dust, glass, and debris I didn't recognize. The happy crowds had vanished, replaced by frightened, angry people who were examining the wreckage of their homes. One of them was Carrie Kimberly.

"Meg, isn't it awful? All those people said it was perfectly safe—that nothing bad would happen. I think every brick chimney in town fell down at once, and the rocks are still falling." She let out a sob. "My church lost all of its stained glass windows." Then she really looked at me. "Meg, are you okay? You look like the bomb exploded right on top of you!"

She nearly had that right. "Carrie, you must help. Out near the bombsite, Freddy Gower was shot. He and Artie were taken away in a helicopter. Probably by someone connected with the project, but I don't really know. Please tell everyone you see."

"Freddy shot? Is he hurt bad?"

"I don't know. I don't know anything. Right now, I've got to find Ethel. Could you just tell everyone about Freddy?"

Ethel was not in the schoolyard or the park. I asked a few people I recognized, but they hadn't seen her. They had glazed eyes, were covered in dust like me, and looked as if they were in a war zone. In a way, I guess we all were. I didn't tell them about Freddy. I trusted Carrie to take on that task. I went home.

"Ethel," I called out.

"In here," she yelled from the kitchen.

I found her shedding angry tears, surrounded by broken dishes. "My grandmother's china," she said. "No one warned us about things falling out of the cabinets. Move the furniture away from the windows, just in case, they said."

"Ethel, I'll help you clean up later. Something's happened. Something bad. We have to find Hal and Walt."

"My boys. Where are they?"

Quickly, I explained what had happened. "Perhaps Freddy wasn't hurt badly. He was able to climb into the helicopter." I waited for her to blame me for not intervening, but she didn't.

Instead she said, "Thank God you followed them. If you hadn't, no one would know anything." I expected hysteria from her. Instead, she was expressionless, in a state of shock. "We must find them." She opened a drawer and removed a small pistol.

"I don't think that's a good idea," I said.

"Well, I do."

Arguing was useless, but I needed to watch her carefully. I suggested we hike to the viewing area. "Hal and Walt might have left already, and we might see them coming back or meet someone who knows where they are."

We traveled along the damaged road, past protestors carrying signs. Not one of them looked any different from us, although the local papers later described them as radical, long-haired hippies.

I asked Ethel why she hadn't been invited to the viewing tent. "Well, I was, but I decided I should look out for our property. I heard the countdown from WKRT in Grand Junction. Just like it was the blast-off to the moon and Neil Armstrong was going to walk down First Street and plant the flag."

She chattered on a bit, and I encouraged her. Anything to keep us moving without thinking too much. We were aware suddenly of a lone car coming down the road. Even from a distance, Ethel could tell it was Hal's. She stepped into the middle of the road, gesturing frantically. Hal stopped the car, and both men hurried over to us.

"What a blast," Hal crowed. "What a damned powerful blast!"

"Wasn't it great, Meg?" I didn't respond to Walt. "Why, what's the matter?"

Ethel whirled on her husband. "You find my boys, Hal Gower. You find them safe and sound and bring them back to me, or don't you ever come home again!"

We explained what had happened on the way back to the house. Walt lashed out at me. "I don't believe this! You were there?"

"I followed them."

Ethel roared to my defense. "And what if she hadn't, Walt Jeffreys? We might never know what happened to our boys!"

"Oh, I'm sure . . ." Walt began, and then he stopped—and stared. We had come to town, and he saw the havoc for the first time.

"You're sure?" I screamed at him. "Are you really sure about anything?"

"Blaming Meg! She could have been shot, too!"

Hal had remained quiet, still trying to process what he'd been told. "Someone shot Freddy, and someone else took our boys away? Walt, you said . . . How could that happen?"

"I'll make some phone calls and find out where they are," Walt said.

I shook my head. "Look around, Walt. You think the phones are working? Do you think anything in Grand Valley is working?"

It seemed as if the whole town had gathered on the Gowers' front lawn. Ruth, Carrie, and Ron Johanssen had done a good job broadcasting the boys' disappearance.

"Why are they here?" Walt asked nervously.

As soon as we got out of the car, they began yelling at him. Some were demanding to know who would fix their property, but most people expressed worry about the Gower boys. "Freddy! Freddy! Freddy!" They began to chant, and I started to worry the situation would turn violent.

Walt shouted over them. "I'm sure Freddy is fine. Just give me a chance to make some phone calls!"

Ruth snorted. "Good luck with that. Your perfectly safe little explosion knocked out the phone lines. No one is going to be calling anyone for some time to come."

"Freddy! Freddy! Freddy!" The crowd continued. Pastor Ron tried to calm them down, but Walt just shrugged and got back into the car.

"We'll drive to Rifle," Hal said. "Perhaps the phones are working there." He moved toward Ethel and held out his arms to comfort her, but she turned her head.

"You bring back my boys, and we'll see," she said. I felt sorry for Hal, who had been taken in by the AEC's promises, too.

"Wait," Ruth said. "Someone is coming." Another car came down the street.

A strange man was driving, but his passenger was Doc Moore. Doc hurried over to Hal and Ethel. "Phone call came in at the police station in Rifle. Your boys are at St. Mary's in Grand Junction. Freddy's badly hurt. Paul Lindstrom will fly us there in his Piper Cub."

Ethel turned to me. "Go, Ethel," I said. "Ruth and I will take care of everything here." She and Hal climbed into Paul's car.

Pastor Ron encouraged the citizens to return home. "Take care of each other. We'll let you know once we receive any news."

Walt remained in the car. Once the crowd had dispersed, he opened the window. "Meg..."

He looked lost. A part of me wanted to reach out to him, but I wasn't ready. "I have to straighten up. I promised Ethel." He didn't say anything. "What will you do, Walt?"

"I'm not sure. I have to find a working phone. I guess I'll drive to Grand Junction—check on Freddy, and leave the car for Hal."

"That would be good. The pilot might not be able to wait for them. Then what will you do?"

"Fly to Denver, I guess. Or maybe to Washington. Depends on what I find out when I make the calls. I'll be in touch, Meg."

I didn't reply. I may have nodded. I followed Ruth into the kitchen.

Halfheartedly, we started picking up pieces of broken china. "You wanted to go to Grand Junction with him," Ruth said. "Why didn't you?"

I sighed. "You're wrong—I don't want to be with him, but I do want to see Freddy. Above all, I must find my family." The tears started. "I just don't know what to do next."

Ruth patted my shoulder and made soothing noises. She wasn't the demonstrative type normally. The earlier hug had been out of character. "Ron told me about your father, and how he came to meet him. It is possible I did him an injustice."

I was grateful Ron had told her about Dad because it was not my story to tell. "I don't know what to think anymore. I'm beginning to question everything I ever knew about my life."

We gave up on the broken dishes. They were shattered beyond repair. Ruth found two mugs still intact and made us tea. I decided I had to tell someone. "Ruth, I saw my father near the viewing area." I described what I'd seen.

"You were far away, Meg. It could have been someone who looked like him."

"Yes, it could have been, but it wasn't. I need to call that hotel in Washington again. I know Dad isn't there, but maybe my mother and brother are. I thought of calling the police, but what police—in what town?"

"Let's ask Ron's advice," Ruth suggested. "You do need to find a working phone. I don't think I'm up to driving around the debris, but he might be willing to take us to Grand Junction."

"Thanks, Ruth. That's a good idea. And maybe we should see how much damage was done to his church and the school . . ." Our mouths dropped, we stared at each other. School! "We're supposed to teach tomorrow!"

"Not going to happen," Ruth said. "Let's go there first."

"And to think I left home less than two weeks ago," I said.

"But it feels like years. I know. Time can be like that. Let's go."

"Maybe we should wash our faces first," I said, wondering if mine was as dirty as Ruth's. We looked at each other and burst out laughing.

"At least we still have our sense of humor," she said.

The school was deserted, but we found Mr. Owens wandering around the disheveled building as if he didn't quite know what to do.

"Ruth and Miss Shaw." He seemed pleased to see us. "Any news yet about Freddy?"

"No," I said, "but without phone service, Hal and Ethel can't let us know."

Mr. Owens shook his head. "This is unbelievable."

"We just came to check the damage and to find out what we're going to do about school for the rest of the week," Ruth said.

"I'm not finding any widespread damage, although things really look a mess. Everyone did a good job of preparing for the blast." He shook his head, correcting himself. "Not that any of us could have been prepared for what happened. Shattered glass, shingles off the roof, cracks in the foundation, but they might have been there already, at least those in the older part."

"The school board will claim they weren't." Ruth's prediction proved correct. More than a few groups and families put in claims for damage that predated Project Rulison.

"Caroline Tucker certainly will," Mr. Owens said.

That name again. Tucker. The school board member my mother thought might be using me for a lure.

"What about school?" Ruth asked. "The kids may be needed at home."

"And their parents might want to keep them safe," I added. Closing school would give us more time also to search for my family and to determine Freddy's condition.

Then the light flickered and died. No electricity made it definite. No school.

We offered to locate a few people who would spread the word that school would stay closed for the remainder of the week. Mr. Owens thanked us and returned to his office.

"Doesn't he want to go home?"

"Ray doesn't have much of one. He rents a room in town. His wife left him awhile back. I doubt he cares much about possessions."

"How sad." There was nothing more to say except . . . "What about your husband, Ruth?"

"Same story as Ray's. Only in my case, the day George left was the happiest of my life. Let's get over to church now."

Reluctantly, Pastor Ron shook his head at our request. He was swamped with people needing both physical and mental comfort. That day was out, but he promised to take us to Grand Junction the following.

Ruth decided to return to school. "If the electricity returns, I'll run off some 'No School' flyers and have some of the older students deliver them. Otherwise, I'll dash off hand-written notes. Good thing we don't have many students and that they don't live far apart. Funny how we've become so dependent on ditto machines and telephones." I offered to help, but she said I should go back home and rustle up something for us to eat.

"Was your house damaged, Ruth?"

"Oh, I got lucky. Just have a lot of dusting to do. I'll make quick work of the flyers and meet you at the Gowers'."

At least one good thing had come out of that fateful day. The least likely person had become my friend. But I had another friend in town, whether or not she wished me to be. Soon, I would check up on Loreen.

Chapter Fifteen

From habit, I reached for the light switch in the kitchen. Oh, right, no power. At least the sun hadn't set completely. In Colorado, unlike Illinois, when the sun goes down it's exactly as if someone had flipped a switch. Light to darkness instantly. Flipped a switch. I shuddered at my inadvertent thought.

Quickly, I used the remaining daylight to search for flashlights, batteries, and a few candles. Then I pulled various salads as well as butter from the refrigerator. Rolls, Cokes, and cookies would complete the meal. Waiting for Ruth, I let it all catch up with me: the terrible destruction, Freddy hurt, Mom, Todd, Dad . . . missing . . .

And Ruth was shining a flashlight into my eyes. Several candles were a-glow. "Suppertime, sleepyhead."

"Oh, Ruth. It's still today?"

"Longest day we've ever had. Food looks good, but let me fix some coffee."

"I didn't know if it was safe to use the stove."

"Gas. Should be." She lit the pilot light.

The freshly perked coffee did make a difference. So did the food. Ruth told me two high school girls would distribute her hand-written notes, saying there would be no school for the rest of the week. We worried together about Freddy and came up with possible scenarios for my family's whereabouts—some absurd—but nothing could be done before morning. Ruth did not stay long. With a flashlight beaming the way, I climbed the stairs and collapsed onto my bed, where I fell into the deepest sleep of my life.

Daylight and downpour came together. Rain was rare in Western Colorado that time of year, but we seemed to be having a lot lately. I hoped it would settle some of the dust and clear the air a bit. There were odd noises downstairs. Could Ethel and Hal be home? I grabbed a robe and rushed downstairs to find Ruth making coffee.

"Breakfast is just cereal," she said. "Still no power. We don't want to open the refrigerator too often, so we'll just dump the milk when we're done."

"Have you seen Ron? Do you know when we'll be going to Grand Junction?"

"He says about noon. We'll get a hot lunch there and then go to the hospital, where you can use the phone and see Freddy. Ron is arranging for a town meeting tonight to show we're all here for each other."

"Does he have time to drive us?"

"If he's needed here, he'll return for us later. It will work out, Meg."

That was easy for her to say, but I sipped my coffee and nodded.

"I'm going back to the church to help figure out how we're going to let everyone know about the meeting. But Meg, if you go out, be careful." She pointed to an extra raincoat and a bandana she'd brought. "Cover your nose and mouth. This rain has me worried. Probably okay, but I'm afraid it might be caused by the explosion, rather than nature tending to its business. Keep the windows closed and stay inside as much as possible."

We planned to meet later at church, but I had no intention of remaining inside. First, I loaded a waterproof bag with some of Freddy's picture books, coloring paper, and crayons, and then added a package of cookies and several apples. Loreen would get help whether or not she wanted it.

Broken windows greeted me. Loreen must not have opened them. Watching where I stepped, I rapped on the door.

"What do you want?" Loreen was holding a baby while two small children peeked out from behind her.

"I'm going to help you."

"I don't want your help."

"I know you don't." I turned my attention to the oldest child, whom I recognized. "Hello. I'm a teacher at your school. Your teacher, Miss Kimberly, is a friend of mine. What's your name?"

"Jana," she said shyly.

Loreen and I exchanged a quick look. When we were nine, we made lists of what we might name our daughters someday. Typically, boys' names never interested us. Jana was always number one on Loreen's list.

"That's a beautiful name," I said. The little girl next to her peeked out. "Could this be Ellen?"

Both youngsters nodded, and Loreen gave a start. Yes, I do remember, I told her silently. "What is your brother's name?" I asked, referring to the baby.

"William," Loreen replied. "Well, get out of the rain, if you're determined to stay. I warn you, it isn't pretty."

No, it wasn't, but then I hadn't expected much. Loreen's home was dirty and bleak and hopeless. At the time, though, I was concerned only with the danger. "We can't have the children going near those glass shards." I held out my arms for the baby, who seemed eager to receive them. He was a friendly, bouncy little fellow.

Reluctantly, Loreen handed him over. "I know that, but I can't clean up the glass and take care of them at the same time."

"That's where I come in. I'll play with the children. But we need a room that doesn't have broken windows."

"My room doesn't." But when Loreen frowned, Jana quickly said, "It's all right, Mommy."

"I've brought things for the children to do."

Loreen gave in and let Jana take us upstairs. "William may need a nap," she cautioned. "Just put him in his crib if he gets cranky."

The bedroom belonged to the two girls, and it was delightfully child-centered and feminine. While I was chatting with Jana and Ellen, William fell asleep. Jana led me to Loreen's bedroom, where William's crib was located, and he went down without a stir. We made a great show of tiptoeing back to the girls' room. Then we sat on a large throw rug while I read Freddy's storybooks. A cookies and apple party followed. "Your mommy and I used to have tea parties when we were your age," I told them.

"You knew my mommy when you were a little girl?" Jana asked, her mouth stuffed with cookies.

"I did, and she always said that someday when she had little girls, their names would be Jana and Ellen." The girls squealed with delight.

"Mine will be Susan," Jana said.

I pretended not to notice Loreen hiding outside the door, listening. When we were through eating our treat, I gave them paper and crayons and left them happily creating works of art.

Downstairs, Loreen was sweeping the remaining glass from the living room floor. "Good thing I never got around to laying carpet in here," she said.

I wanted to say she should keep the children off the floor for some time to come, but I swallowed the warning and said instead, "William is asleep, and the girls are coloring. Your children are adorable, Loreen."

She emptied the glass into a large container. "They're a good bunch. I'll make us some tea, or would you rather have coffee?"

"Tea is fine. Like our old tea parties." I followed her into the kitchen.

"Kathy was your favorite name for a girl," she said, not looking up from the sink where she was scrubbing out a few cups.

"I'm surprised you remember."

"Not as surprised as I am, since you must have put me out of your mind completely."

"Why do you think that?"

"Because I never heard from you again. You didn't write even one letter."

"Loreen, I was only ten-years-old, and my life totally changed overnight. I never ever stopped missing you."

Loreen sipped her tea in silence. Finally—"The first of November when I was ten was one of the saddest days of my life. You broke my heart, Meggy. I didn't have any friends for a long, long time, until Jim came along. Then he abandoned me, too, and I had Jana to raise all by myself."

I didn't ask about the father of her other two children, and I didn't ask about her parents. Somehow I'd known, even back then, her parents were completely different from mine. "And you still resent me?"

"It's not that simple, and I may have some things wrong." She explained, to my horror, that in the last few years she'd heard the reason my family had left was because my father had taken all the money for a project that should have been shared with someone else. "It was the same as theft, he said, and it ruined him."

"That kind of goes along with some of the rumors I've heard. Who is this man?" Silence. "Look, I need to know." I explained the strange circumstances of my being hired at the GV school.

"Milton Tucker," she said. "His wife is on the school board. No one likes them very much, but sometimes when you hear a story over and over..."

"...you start to believe it. I don't know what happened between my father and anyone else. All I know is I'm not my father, and I want people to stop resenting me as if I were." I found it impossible to believe Dad had ever stolen anything.

"And I heard some women talking," Loreen continued. "Two of them were teachers. They said you were planning to take Carrie Kimberly's job away from her."

"Carrie told me about that. I'm a first-year teacher. I don't have any power at all. I told you how I got the job. Oh, I'll admit I was naive. I never questioned it before. Now I'm as puzzled as you are."

Because of our conversation, though, I was becoming less puzzled. Apparently, I *was* a lure, and it was possible I'd been enticed back because of the belief my father would follow me. That may have happened already. I had enemies, and now I knew at least two of their names—Milton and Caroline Tucker.

I put down my empty teacup. It was time to go. "I've enjoyed being with your children. Can we start again, Loreen? With our friendship?"

"We can try," she said, "but our lives have been so different."

"Yes, they have, and until recently, mine has been smooth. But Loreen, you need to know I respect you. Judging from those loving, intelligent, well-behaved children, you are doing a great deal that's right." I left. We both had plenty to think about.

Chapter Sixteen

I HADN'T BEEN TO GRAND JUNCTION since I was a small child and had few memories of it, including how breathtaking the drive was as the road followed the Book Cliffs all the way to Utah. "What I love most," I said to Ruth and Ron from the backseat, "are the different views in all directions: red rocks behind us, mesas to the south, canyons straight ahead, and . . ."

"Book Cliffs to the north," Ron concluded. "I never tire of it. Nothing like it in Illinois is there?"

"Nothing." But I sighed. Illinois sounded good to me then.

"Do you have enough change for the phone, Meg?" Ruth asked.

"I hope so."

"Well, I robbed my piggy bank for you, just in case. Who will you try calling first?"

"The hotel in Washington. And then maybe Libby, depending on the time, although I don't think she'll know anything."

"You'll find a pay phone at the hospital," Ron said. "Then I guess we'll just see . . ."

I retreated into my own thoughts and let them chatter away without me. It hadn't taken long to realize that Ron was not interested in me, at least not romantically. He and Ruth were obviously in love. I just couldn't tell whether or not they knew it themselves. She seemed a lot older than he, but it was none of my business. My business right then was Dad, Mom, Todd, Freddy, and maybe Walt. I sighed again. What was I going to do if my phone calls didn't produce answers?

Again, Ruth homed in on the sigh. She was becoming sensitive to my moods. "Did you get anywhere with Loreen, Meg?"

"I think I made some headway." I explained the relationship to Ron and related my experience that morning.

Ruth shook her head. "She's a prickly one, all right, but she certainly needs help."

"She's had a tragic life," Ron said. "I thought we'd lose her after Will Brackett was killed in that Moab mine collapse before William was born. Could you get her to come to the meeting, Meg? I'm going to encourage people to reach out and help each other—in some kind of organized way."

Ruth snorted. "Not likely she'll come. Not without someone to watch those three kids."

"I want to help, but I don't think I can commit to anything—yet." But I had a brainstorm. "I know what might work, though. Ron, could you find some volunteers—maybe high school students, even Betty from my class—to have a little playgroup in your church while the parents attend the meeting? I don't think Loreen would let anyone into her house, but she might bring the kids there. I'm sure we could figure out a way to pay the sitters."

"Meg, that's a wonderful idea," Ron said. "I'll get started on it as soon as I get back. I'll bet the teenagers would be willing to do it without pay. The idea is that we all pitch in and help each other."

"I'll get the babysitters," Ruth said. "You've got enough to do, Ron."

I told them what Loreen had revealed about the Tuckers. Ruth nodded. "I heard old Milt was riled up about something. I doubt if there's any truth to it, but now you're wondering if your father has fallen into some kind of trap Milt has set."

"Yes. It does seem absurd, though."

"Stranger things have happened," Ron said. "Milt is mean enough. I just don't think he's all that smart. Let me think about it. Here we are now in Grand Junction."

After a quick lunch, which wasn't quick enough for me, we arrived at St. Mary's Hospital, where we were directed to a small waiting room and were joined by Hal and Artie. Artie and I looked at each other. Then we were sobbing in each other's arms. "It's bad, Meg. The doctors say he might not make it. Freddy might die."

I could hear Hal discussing the situation with Ruth and Ron—where the bullet had struck, what the prognosis was. But I didn't pay much attention. All that mattered were Artie's words, "Freddy might die."

"May we see him?" I asked.

Hal shook his head. "Not a good idea. He's unconscious. He wouldn't know you were there." Hal seemed to have aged years in less than twenty-four hours. Ethel won't leave his side. He'll need a second operation. All we can do now is wait."

"Could we see Ethel?" Ruth asked.

Again, Hal shook his head. "Not this time. I would like you to take Artie back home, though."

"No!"

"Please, son. You've been a grand help, but it's time to go home."

"I won't leave Freddy."

Doc Moore came into the room and overheard. "We just received a call from Walt Jeffreys. He's in Denver and says we'll need to have photos of the damage in town if the government and oil companies are going to pay for it." At our indignant looks, he added, "Mr. Jeffreys was apologetic. It wasn't his decision. So we need pictures. Do any of you have a camera?"

Artie and I just stared at each other. The camera! How could we have forgotten? I'd snapped erratically and couldn't even remember what I took after Freddy rushed toward the helicopter. It was possible I captured a photo of the shooter. Finally, Artie nodded. "I have a camera. I'll go home."

Ron went to get his car while Ruth tried to comfort Artie. I found a phone booth. The message at the Hay-Adams was simple. They refused to give out any information. Next, I called Libby, but she must not have been home from school; there was no answer. Last, I called home, with the same disappointing, though expected, results.

In the car, I sought advice. "Should I call the police?"

"Which police, Meg? Des Plaines, D.C., or Grand Valley?"

Ruth had a point. "I don't know," I said.

"Are you certain you saw your father?" Ron asked.

"Positive."

"Then I think you must assume he's in the area and will contact you when he can."

I wasn't happy to leave it at that, but I had no other options. At least, not until phone service was restored. "Let's talk about Artie's camera," I said. "The photos I took might reveal something."

"Like who shot Freddy," Artie said.

"We should get the film developed right away."

"I don't know if that's a good idea, Ruth," I said. "We need to be sure we can trust whoever develops it."

Ruth said she knew one of the high school teachers, a man very much against the project, who would surely develop them. "Once there's electricity, of course."

Artie agreed to put a fresh roll of film in the camera and start documenting the damage in town while Ruth and I helped Ron with the town meeting and playroom preparations. We needed to work fast.

We were silent the rest of the way home. We hadn't come up with anything definite to find my family or help Freddy, but at least we had a plan for the rest of that day.

A welcoming sight greeted us as we drove into town. A light in Hannah's Sandwich. Electricity! Three of us cheered, but Artie gasped. "Oh, no!"

He hadn't seen the destruction before. The rest of us had adjusted somewhat, but it was new and shocking to him. We looked at Grand Valley again through Artie's eyes while Ron drove carefully to avoid glass and bricks on the road. The front porch had disappeared from my student Mike's house. Most of the houses had cracks in their foundations and missing shingles from the roofs. Tumbleweeds continued to blow everywhere, and even the trees and bushes were coated in dust and grime. We drove into the cracked remains of the Gower driveway. "Get my camera now, Meg," Artie demanded.

Chapter Seventeen

Artie removed the film from the camera and handed it to Ruth, before loading a fresh roll and hurrying off.

"This is a good thing for him. He needs a mission," Ruth said.

"The only reason Artie left Freddy was because Walt requested those photos," Ron said. We promised to meet him later at the church.

I must have reacted to Walt's name, for once we were alone, Ruth said, "Walt Jeffreys. What about him, Meg?"

"I don't know what you mean."

"Yes you do."

I shook my head. "Why don't you ask me something easy? I was beginning to care, but I'm not sure I can trust him." I told her what Ethel had told me—that Walt had known who my father was before he met me but pretended great surprise when I told him.

"Be careful, Meg. Watch what you do with your heart."

"And what about you, Ruth? What about you and Ron?"

"Still figuring that one out. Tell you what. I'll change the subject if you do."

"It's a deal. Now you'd better take that film to your friend."

I was freshening up when I heard the most wonderful sound. The telephone! My heart started racing. Could it be Dad or news about

Freddy? I rushed down to the kitchen and picked up the phone just in time.

"Hello?"

"Meg, it's Walt." Surprisingly, the last person I expected. I didn't say anything. "Are you there?"

"Yes, sorry. We just got the phones back. How are you?"

"I'm not sure. Just listen. This is important. I'll be driving over this evening from Denver with claim forms for the residents who had damage to their property."

"Good. About the claim forms, I mean." I wasn't so sure how good it was he was coming.

"I'm going to need photographs."

"Artie is out taking them now."

"Artie isn't in Grand Junction?"

"No, Hal talked him into coming home."

"Any news about Freddy?"

"No." I heard the telltale clicks of the party line. Someone being nosy, or one of my supposed enemies? Impossible to say. "I should get going, Walt."

"Tell Artie not to bother getting the roll of pictures developed. I'll handle it." I didn't respond. "I'm thinking about you, Meg."

"I know." I didn't trust myself to say more. I hung up, my hand shaking. Don't think about him, I told myself. Walt was not a priority, but my family was. I needed to call Libby.

"Meggy!" she shrieked. "What's going on? Why haven't you called me?"

There was too much to tell. "The telephone service was out. A lot has been happening here. But, Libby, I'm calling about my family. Did you find out anything?"

"Nothing. I've driven by your house a dozen times at least, and Todd hasn't been in school all week. Do you want me to call that Washington hotel again?"

"Thanks, Libby, but I called already. They're not there. I'm not sure what to do next."

"I asked your neighbors. They don't know anything, either. But your mom cancelled newspaper and milk delivery, so I guess they meant to go away."

"I guess so," I said. "I don't know whether to be scared or angry."

Libby wrote down the Gowers' phone number and promised to call if she learned anything.

A few hours passed. It was too hard to stay in the house with nothing for company but troubling thoughts, so I went over to church to see if I could help.

"Meg." Ruth grabbed me. "Parents are showing up in droves with their children. See if you can help sign them in."

"I need to see you about the photos, Meg."

"Would you be able to seat people, Meg?"

Requests seem to be coming from all over. Suddenly, I had become popular. "Ron, I'm sorry. Ruth asked first for help registering the children. Artie, come and help me, and we'll be able to talk about the photos sooner."

Well, I wouldn't call it a mob, but the noise level was pretty high. Twelve children, a few carrying stuffed animals, had arrived. The youngest was Loreen's William and the oldest my student Betty, who would be a tremendous help. Two young moms were in charge. Artie and I had the parents sign a list with their children's names, and the mothers and the older students corralled the children into age-appropriate activities. I overheard the mothers wondering if they might turn this effort into something full time—a job for them and a service for Grand Valley parents. Perhaps, in some strange way, I had managed to accomplish something for this unfortunate community.

The only awkward moment came when Ruth escorted an older woman and her toddler grandson into the room and insisted on introducing me. "Mrs. Tucker, this is Margaret Shaw, the new teacher. The playroom was Miss Shaw's idea."

Caroline Tucker scarcely looked at me. "Just make sure you take good care of Martin," she said, before rushing out.

I shrugged. "That's the woman who wanted me to apply here," I said to Artie. At least one of my enemies now had a face.

Artie and I found an empty room where we could talk uninterrupted. He told me he had gone to every house and business in town and had taken photos of whatever damage the owners planned to report. "Walt said he'd get the photos developed," I said.

"I was afraid of that," Artie said, "and I wish I could trust him to do the right thing, but I don't. So . . ." He paused and grinned at me. "I borrowed a friend's camera and took duplicates of everything. I will have those developed. We'll have a set, and so will Walt. So no monkey business!" He sounded exactly like his mother.

"The ones I'm longing to see are those Ruth is having her friend develop."

"Yes. She said he should have them for us tomorrow and would make several copies of each. We'll be careful about which photos we give Walt."

"The meeting will start soon," I said. "Let's go upstairs."

"Right. 'Solidarity Forever'!"

I stared at him. Was this the right moment? Would there ever be a better time? "Let's wait a bit. I want to talk to you about something." I patted the chair beside me.

"Okay . . . Is it about Freddy?"

"No, this is about you, Artie. I don't know anyone your age or even years older who has ever used the slogan, 'Solidarity Forever'."

"We're interested in unions out here."

"Not a good enough answer. Artie, you've got to realize how smart you are."

"So?" He gave me his old stubborn, belligerent face.

"So you should be in high school, not deliberately lagging behind to be with Freddy."

"He needs me—maybe now more than ever."

"Of course he does, and you need him. You're best friends as well as brothers. But aren't there better ways of helping other than failing in school? Have you thought about the future? Is society going to be blessed with two uneducated men, who can't find decent jobs and aren't able to support themselves? Your parents won't be able to provide for you your whole lives."

"I don't understand."

"Sure you do, or if you don't, try harder. Freddy has Down Syndrome. He will learn what he can, but he's not a likely candidate for the honor roll. People will always love him, though, for the kind, affectionate person he is. He'll be fine in school without you. You don't see people making fun of him, but if they did, I'll bet he'd start laughing along with them. They would soon see the error of their ways."

"But if I pass him by, won't he feel bad?"

"Freddy doesn't think that way. He thinks he's just fine the way he is, and he doesn't get his feelings hurt easily. It would never occur to him to be jealous of you. He may be older and larger, but you're really the big brother. You need to learn as much as you can—for your sake and for Freddy's. You might be his financial support someday. How is that going to work with only a grade school education?"

Artie nodded gravely, and I gave an inward sigh. He understood. I'd gotten through to him. "What do you think I should do?"

"Let's talk to Mrs. Arnold. If you work hard, maybe you'll be able to transfer in January. I'm sure there would be tests you would need to pass first."

He stood. "I'll think about it. Thanks. I'll see you upstairs."

I heard soft applause, and Ruth came into the room. "Bravo!"

"Now if only Freddy is okay."

"Yes. We'll call the hospital after the meeting. You coming up?"

"Just give me a minute, Ruth." I didn't care whether or not I went to the meeting. I closed my eyes and sat awhile longer, not even thinking.

"Meggy, are you okay?"

I didn't recognize the voice. How long had I been sitting there? I opened my eyes. "Oh, Loreen, it's you. I'm fine—just resting. I think I might have fallen asleep."

"Thanks to you, that's what I'm going to do tomorrow."

"Oh?" Was she being sincere or sarcastic?

"The playroom. They're going to call it the Children's Center. Clara and Gail told me it was your idea. It's going to be everyday but Sunday now, and it doesn't cost too much. My kids had a great time. Tomorrow, I'm going to get some rest. Then I'm going to figure out how to get a job and maybe even my GED. So, thanks. I'm going to take them home now. They're so excited, I hope I can get them to sleep."

"But the meeting?"

She laughed. "Oh, that's over. Mrs. Arnold said I should let you sleep. I did for a while, but we need to leave, and I wanted to thank you."

"I'm glad it's working out for you, Loreen, but I just had the idea. Other people did the work."

"Meg. Excuse me for interrupting, Mrs. Brackett. Meg, Walt's here. Uh—people aren't being very nice to him."

The fool! He should have waited at the house. "I'll come see you soon, Loreen." I dashed out of the room with Artie.

By the time we got back upstairs, Walt was gone, and Ron was soothing an irate crowd. "Let's try to control our anger," he said. "We don't know yet what the government's response will be. We're all unhappy, but we need their help. A little show of cooperation might go a long way." A lot of muttering but most of them nodded as they left the church. They understood Ron's point.

As soon as they left, Ron handed me a clipboard of papers. "Here are the damage claims. I'm keeping copies. Walt is waiting for you at the Gowers' house. He was badly shaken by what happened here."

"He should be," Artie said, "and I don't want him at my house."

"Careful, Art," Ron said. "This isn't Walt's doing, and he's in a terrible position right now."

I, too, needed to keep those words in mind. "He was so certain the test would succeed. You're right, Ron. Probably Walt is more disappointed than anyone."

"That's not going to help my family."

Artie and I left together. "I'll talk to Walt. Why don't you just go to your room and wait for me. Then we'll call the hospital."

"I don't want him staying with us."

"Understood." I didn't say that was up to his parents, though I doubted they'd want Walt around, either.

Walt was standing beside his car in the driveway. Artie ignored him and went inside. "Since you'll stay outside, I'll call the hospital now," he said, his meaning clear.

I handed Walt the clipboard and the roll of film Artie had used to document the town's damages. "We have duplicates of everything."

"Because you don't trust us," Walt said. I didn't respond. "The people here hate me now. Do you?"

I shook my head. "Of course not. This has been awful for you, too."

He gave a sigh of relief and took me into his arms. "You have no idea, Meg." I must have been unresponsive and stiff, for he let go immediately. "You've changed," he said.

"Everyone's changed, and everything's different. I just don't know how much yet. This town has lost its innocence. Don't expect anyone to automatically believe what you say. Grand Valley folks have had their fill of rash, uninformed promises."

"But they weren't rash. Okay, the damages were greater than anticipated."

"Anticipated? You weren't anticipating any! Move the furniture away from the windows and stay outside. That was the best you could do?"

"You're right. We should have known better—and prepared the citizens better, but the natural gas is there now. There will be jobs for local people and increased energy for the whole country. You'll see . . ."

"Yes, we'll see. First, we'll see if Freddy recovers. Artie says he may die. I can't think beyond that right now. Someone shot him—remember?"

"Of course I remember. I wouldn't have had that happen for the world. What about your family, Meg? Have you heard from your father?"

"No." I wasn't about to discuss my family. Because the biggest thing that had changed for me was trust. I no longer trusted him. And sadly, without that, we had nothing.

"I have to drive back to Denver tonight—to deliver these claims."

"Do you think the government will honor them?"

"I don't know." At least he was honest.

He bent over to kiss me. I still liked him more than any man I'd ever met, and I might have let him, but just then another car pulled into the driveway. We watched a young man get out.

"Meggy?"

"Todd? Is that you?"

My six-foot-two big little brother wrapped his arms around me—something he hadn't done in years. "Meggy, I didn't know where else to go."

Chapter Eighteen

Walt and Todd did not take to each other. I expected Walt to leave immediately, but he just stood there in the driveway, at first making small talk, and then trying to get Todd to talk about my father. I couldn't believe how insensitive he was. Finally I said, "Walt, Todd is exhausted. I need to take him inside. Don't you think you should go? You've got a long drive ahead."

"Oh, of course." Walt came toward me as if for a goodnight kiss—in front of my brother whom he'd just met. I stepped back. "Goodbye then. It was nice meeting you, Todd."

The two switched cars around, and Walt was on his way. "He asks too many questions," Todd said, as we entered the kitchen. "Who is he, Meggy? I don't think I like him."

"You're not the only one." It was Artie. I introduced them, and Artie quickly discerned that we needed to talk alone. "No change with Freddy, Meg. He's still unconscious. I'll fix up the guest room for Todd and see you later."

"Nice kid," Todd said.

"The best. Sit down, and I'll fix you something to eat. And then I need to hear everything. Especially about Mom and Dad."

Todd looked ready to drop, so I knew he wasn't going to be able to talk for long. I scrambled some eggs, which he devoured. Then—"Who was that man, Meggy?"

"His name is Walter Jeffreys. He works for the Atomic Energy Commission." I told Todd a little about what had been happening in Grand Valley.

"They exploded a nuclear bomb? You're kidding me, right?" As I had suspected, the media hadn't covered Project Rulison. At least, not east of Denver.

"I wish I were."

"Crazy. Is that why the roads were such a mess? It was too dark to see much."

"I'll tell you all about it tomorrow. Right now, you need to tell me what's happened to you. And where are Mom and Dad?"

Todd sighed. "I wish I knew. It all started right after we talked. I'm not sure when that was now. I hung up because I thought Mom was home. But it wasn't her. It was Libby."

"I know."

"Then I got another call," Todd continued. "I thought it might be you calling back, but it wasn't. It was pretty scary. At the time I thought it was a crank call . . ."

But it hadn't been. The caller told Todd that if Dad didn't stop meddling, none of his family would be safe. "You got a threatening phone call?"

"And another one the next morning. From the same person, I think." By that time, Todd had been so unnerved he almost didn't answer the next call that came. "Good thing I did. It was Mom."

"Did she tell you where she was?"

"No. She said she couldn't talk long but that I was to leave the house immediately and find a safe place to stay until she could find a way of getting in touch with me."

"But how would she do that unless she knew where you were?"

"She was talking so fast, I didn't think to ask. She told me where she had money hidden—that I should take it, some keys from Dad's desk drawer, and get in her car and go."

"Did you tell her about the threatening phone calls?"

"Meggy, she didn't give me a chance to tell her anything. She hung up after she told me to take her car." Todd's eyes welled up. His experiences had been worse than mine. At least I hadn't always been alone.

"You're with me now," I said. "It's going to be okay. What did you do next?"

Todd found the Washington D.C. phone number on a pad next to Mom's bed and took it downstairs to make the call from the kitchen, which is where Libby had discovered it. "It was a hotel," he said.

I nodded. "The Manger Hay-Adams. Did you get through to them?"

"No, the person at the desk said they weren't available. So I found the money and keys and packed some stuff and drove to Washington."

"Todd, you drove to Washington D.C.? You haven't had your license long enough to do that. What was the traffic like?"

"Awful, but I didn't know where else to go." By the time he arrived, our parents had checked out without leaving a forwarding address. "So I decided to come here."

My little brother had driven more than 2000 miles all by himself, eating at truck stops, staying overnight at flea-bitten motels where he didn't think he'd be questioned. "Todd, I'm so proud of you," I said. He might have been foolish, but he was also very brave.

"There's more. When I was going through Glenwood Canyon, someone driving a small truck tried to run me off the road."

I gasped. "Are you sure?"

"Oh, yes, and would have succeeded if a farmer driving a tractor hadn't come along. Whoever it was lost his nerve and took off."

It was late. Todd couldn't take much more, and neither could I. I took him to the guest room and then peeked in on Artie, fast asleep on his bed—still dressed, with the lights on. I threw a comforter over him and turned out the lights. The two longest days of my life were over.

The phone woke me from a restless sleep. I raced to the kitchen, but Artie beat me to it. "Hello, Dad? Yes. Yes. That's great! Don't worry, I'll figure out a way! Okay. Bye." Artie gave me a huge smile and began to cry.

"Freddy?"

"He woke up!"

"And he's okay?"

"Well, they don't know that yet, but they think he might be. I need to go see him."

"Of course."

Artie fetched Todd as I fixed a quick breakfast for the three of us. We decided to go to the church to see if Ron could drive us back to Grand Junction.

Another person was in Ron's study when we arrived. "Ruth," I said, very pleased to see her. I introduced Todd and could tell they were going to like each other. We related the good news about Freddy.

Ron reached for the phone. "I saw Ray Owens earlier. He's driving over to Grand Junction this morning. I'm sure he'll take you, Art." Ron made the call, and Artie rushed out to join the principal at the school.

A part of me wanted to go with Artie, but the time was long past to deal with my family's problems. "Now, Todd," I said. "Tell what happened to you."

When he was done, Ruth frowned. "The whole story is preposterous. Let's start with the attempt on your life—for that's what being driven off the road in Glenwood Canyon amounts to. I assumed

Milt Tucker was behind all your troubles, but that doesn't sound like him."

"I agree," Ron said. "Besides, he doesn't drive anymore. What about Caroline? Could the driver have been a woman?"

Todd didn't think so.

"Doesn't sound like her either," Ruth said. "She is opinionated and has a nasty tongue in her mouth, but I don't think she'd do anything violent."

"It must have something to do with Dad and why he's missing." I told Todd of the different rumors about Dad—what Loreen had said and Rispa Moore and, of course, Milton Tucker.

"That's crazy. Dad can be secretive sometimes, but he's honest. Why do you think he went to Washington?"

"I can think of two possibilities," Ron said. "Chet might have been testifying in favor of the nuclear test or against it. I'm guessing he was one of the people who opposed it."

"In spite of his being a mining engineer?" Todd seemed skeptical.

Ron filled Todd in on where he met Dad. "After all the work he did on the project, he concluded it would fail. That the gas would be unsafe to use."

"So what do we know?" Ruth asked. "We know your parents were in Washington at a particular hotel, but aren't there now. What we don't know is if they are still in Washington."

"Perhaps there was no reason for Chet to stay," Ron said. "The Supreme Court refused to hear testimony. The case was dropped. It never had a chance, really."

"And you're forgetting I saw Dad in the viewing area."

"I don't know, Meg. You weren't close. It could have been someone who looked like him."

"No," Todd said. "If Meg said it was him, it was. Even if it were far away, she'd know our dad. And he's got to be somewhere. Why not here?"

"Then where is he now?"

"It's time to start asking questions," Ron said. "We need to be careful, but we should visit both the Tuckers and the Moores. There must be a good reason all this is happening. Let's find out what it is."

Ruth nodded. "Ron, could you drive us to Rifle to see the Moores? I don't think we should use Todd's mother's car. Too risky, all things considered, and I'm leery of driving on torn-up roads."

Ron had to keep a few appointments first. "But I'll call Doc Moore and find out what time would be best."

"And I need to see if the photos are ready," Ruth said. I was anxious to see them and dreaded it at the same time. It was possible one would reveal who shot Freddy.

Todd and I put together a shopping list. Because of the power failure, we needed to buy fresh food in Rifle. Then I took Todd on a brief tour of Grand Valley, to see the school and, of course, the terrible damage to the town.

"Photos?" I asked Ruth later, when we met at the church. She shook her head. Maybe later in the day.

And the day was crisp and gorgeous. Soon the leaves would add some needed color to sandstone and dusty gray. I longed to see the golden aspen leaves and hoped to appreciate them when I did. We drove by Anvil Points. Todd couldn't remember living there but was curious about his first home. We would return at a later time, when everything was settled, I promised. When we passed the vanadium mill in its new location west of Rifle, I asked Ruth if she thought there was any connection between the timing of the closing of the original mill and my family leaving Colorado. "Someone suggested the closing had something to do with my father," I added.

"That would be to your father's credit. He made the case that the old mill was outmoded and suggested the upgrades on the new location."

"Did you ever meet my father?" Todd asked.

"Never had the pleasure," Ruth said, "and it's quite likely it would have been a pleasure."

"Let's hope you meet both our parents," I said.

"Try to remember where you heard Dad was to blame for closing the mill," Todd said. "It could be important."

I shook my head. "Maybe it was Loreen."

"It seems to me," Ruth said, "that Chet Shaw ended up being a convenient scapegoat for anything troublesome that happened around that time."

"We did leave suddenly, and Anvil Points closed soon after." I couldn't get around that fact.

"I've told you what I think. Your father saw the end coming. He must have received a good offer at just the right time."

I hoped Ron was right, but that didn't explain why we couldn't even say goodbye to our friends and why we never knew what Dad's new job was. I could almost see Todd thinking the same things. We looked at each other and shook our heads.

After a quick lunch and an even quicker food shopping expedition, we left our car parked on the street and walked to the Moores' house. Doc Moore was as friendly as ever, exclaiming how Todd had grown and insisting on telling the familiar story —how my parents weren't able to reach the hospital in Glenwood Springs in time, and how Doc Moore delivered Todd in his office. Usually, Todd rolled his eyes, but this was the first time he heard the story from the doctor himself.

Doc Moore gave us an update on Freddy. Even though Freddy had regained consciousness, recovery was still uncertain. "As soon as he stabilizes, it might be necessary to transfer him to a hospital in Denver." I wondered what the Gowers would do if that happened.

The atmosphere changed once Rispa Moore joined us in the living room. She was pleasant to Ron and Ruth but ignored Todd and me. "Now, what is this all about?" she demanded.

"Go ahead, Meg," Ron prompted.

I took a deep breath. "I overheard you saying my father should be in jail. I should have questioned you right then and there, but I was too much of a coward."

"You were shocked, Meg. You were their guest and didn't know how to react." I smiled at Ruth for understanding.

"That may be, but Todd and I need Mrs. Moore to tell us now."

"Todd's and Meg's parents are missing, and we'd appreciate any help you might give us," Ron said.

"We're both really scared," Todd said.

It was Todd's comment, I thought, that softened Rispa.

She hesitated. "It was just something I heard."

"Tell them, Rispa," Doc said.

"Well, it might have been just a rumor, now that I think about it, but..."

"What? Please tell us. My parents could be in danger; my brother was nearly killed."

Doc Moore took over. "The rumor is that Chet Shaw is a Communist and sold secrets about the vanadium mill to the Russians."

"Someone was in Denver and heard he went to a meeting that was full of Communists," Rispa added.

"Then, Mrs. Moore, you'll need to start calling me a Communist, too, because I was at that meeting. That was where I met Charles Shaw."

"You, Pastor Johanssen?" The Moores stared at Ron.

"There might have been some Communists attending, but I'm not one, and neither is Chet Shaw. It was a gathering of people opposing

Project Plowshare because of the harm we believed it would cause the environment. Chet was one of the speakers."

"But I thought he was one of the originators of the tests," Doc Moore said.

"He was," Ron said, "but his studies concluded that the explosions would be dangerous and the natural gas resulting would be too contaminated to use."

"And it's beginning to look as if someone wanted him to keep his findings to himself," Ruth said grimly.

"Honestly, Mrs. Moore, our father is not a Communist," Todd said.

She wasn't quite willing to give in. "Then what about Sputnik?"

"Sputnik?" We stared at her.

"That's right. The Russians launched Sputnik just before you took off so suddenly."

Ruth burst out laughing. "Rispa, listen to yourself. Next you'll be saying Chet Shaw shot JFK!"

There was a long pause, and Mrs. Moore finally spoke. "I'm sorry. I should know better than to listen to idle chatter."

"I'm sorry, too," Doc Moore said. "I should have stopped the gossip each time I heard it, but . . ."

". . . but we did leave suddenly, and you didn't know what to think," I finished for him. Doc Moore nodded.

"Okay, now what?" Todd asked, as soon as we left Doc and Rispa.

We could return to Grand Valley and question Caroline and Milton Tucker—Ruth's suggestion, and I agreed. But Ron said he thought the old man would be drunk by then. "He'll be more alert tomorrow morning." I sighed. So much waiting!

Then Todd suggested we do something for fun.

"That might make a nice change," I said. "How about Rifle Falls? I've wanted to see it again."

"Should be beautiful this time of year," Ruth said, "and a break from so much seriousness might be just what we need."

Todd and I climbed into the back seat. Ruth leaned over to take her place next to Ron when she suddenly cried out in pain. "My ankle!"

"What happened?"

"A pothole. I didn't see it. Oh, drat!"

Ron thought we should return to Doc Moore's, but Ruth refused. She thought all she needed was rest. "I'm sure it's nothing."

None of us wanted to go back to the Moores, so we went along with Ruth's wishes.

The drive to the falls was farther than I remembered. The twisting, turning road was unpaved, so the ride was uncomfortable, especially for Ruth. She seemed pale, and I thought her ankle must bother her, although she denied it. We were miles away from Rifle, and clouds were rolling in fast. We would soon lose our beautiful day.

"Maybe we should turn back," I said to Ron.

"Not yet," he said, holding tightly to the steering wheel.

"Is something wrong?"

"I don't know yet. That car behind us—I don't like the way it's acting."

"What's it doing?" Todd asked.

Both he and I turned to look. "Try to see who is driving," I said.

A car that Todd identified as a 1965 Buick moved parallel to ours and began to edge us closer and closer to the side of the road. Up ahead, we could see a sheer-drop cliff. If we kept on going, that would be our fate.

"Stop the car, Ron!" I yelled. "Stop the car right now!"

"What?" He was distracted but, fortunately, followed my directions. The Buick went on a bit and then stopped, too.

From a distance, I had seen a farmer's truck coming up the road. The driver of the Buick saw it, too, and sped out of sight.

"That's what happened to me in Glenwood Canyon," Todd said.

"Almost, but not quite. I recognized the driver."

"Who was he, Meg?" Ron's voice shook.

"I don't know his name, but we can find out. He was one of the men who spoke to us about the project. He's either in the AEC or from Austral Oil."

"And he tried to kill us," Todd said. "Let's turn around, Ron. Let's go straight back to Grand Valley."

Ron shook his head and put his hand on Ruth's forehead. "We'll see Doctor Moore first."

"Ruth?" I shook her shoulder gently. No answer. "Ruth, are you all right?"

Ron looked back at me, fearfully, his heart in his eyes. "She fainted back when the Buick started shoving us. Between that and her ankle, it was too much."

Well, I guess Ron knows now he's in love with Ruth, I thought.

Chapter Nineteen

Doc Moore insisted that Ruth be taken directly to Rifle's new, small hospital. She protested, of course. "Stop all this fuss! I'm fine. Please take me home, Ron." But she winced again, and I saw her bite back tears.

"Out of the question," Ron said.

It seemed that Rispa had changed her attitude toward us. "No need for all of you to go," she said. "It could be a long wait at the hospital."

Ron would accompany Ruth, but Todd and I would stay with Rispa. I remembered something, probably just in time. "The groceries. Mrs. Moore, may I put the perishables in your refrigerator?"

"Of course you may, and call me Rispa."

Ron seemed relieved they would use Doc Moore's car. He looked almost as worn out as Ruth. No doubt it was starting to dawn on him what a narrow escape we had.

Rispa hustled off to the kitchen to prepare some tea, and the phone rang. She returned immediately. "It's for you," she said. "It's Artie Gower."

I was almost afraid to pick up the receiver. "Let it be good news," I whispered.

But it turned out to be not just about Freddy. "Meg, Dad and I are home. We're doing some packing because we'll be going to Denver as soon as Freddy is well enough for the trip."

"That's wonderful," I said. "How did you know I was here?"

"Ron left a message at the church. We called there. But I'm not calling about Freddy. We got a phone call a few minutes ago from your mother."

"Mom! Where is she? Is she all right?"

"I guess so. She called from Walker Field."

"Mom's in Grand Junction," I whispered to Todd, who had come rushing to the phone. "She called from the airport."

Artie continued. "She sure was glad Todd was with you."

I heard an odd click. The party line was active again. This time, I didn't let it pass. "Look, whoever is listening to this conversation, you need to stop invading people's privacy. Hang up now." I didn't hear a response, so the person was still listening. At least he or she was now on notice. "Artie, let's not say much more. Just keep it simple. But did she say anything about our father?"

"No. She just said she'd find a hotel near the airport and call again later."

"Good. If we're not home, get a phone number from her. I don't know how much longer we'll be here." Quickly, I told him about Ruth's injury. "We don't know whether it's a break or a sprain. I'll let you know when I can." I started to hang up.

"Wait, Meg. Walt called and left a number for you. Do you want it?"

"Not until I'm back home."

"You didn't ask about the photos Ruth's friend developed," Todd said, as soon as I hung up.

"Because someone was listening in, as usual."

"Probably harmless, but you never can tell," Rispa said.

"What about Mom?"

I filled both of them in on what little I knew. "I don't think we'll make it to Grand Junction before tomorrow, but maybe we'll be able to talk to her later, if she leaves a number. At least we know she's safe now."

"I wonder if she knows where Dad is?" I didn't answer, but, of course, that *was* the big question.

Rispa served us a light supper, which we nibbled on, distractedly, waiting for the phone to ring. Several hours passed, while we worried about Ruth as well as Mom and Dad. "Ron was pretty upset," I said.

Rispa chuckled. "That doesn't surprise me a bit."

"How old do you think Ruth is? Fifty, maybe?"

"Heaven's no. Let's see, we went to a surprise birthday party for Ruth only last year. I don't remember what month it was, but she turned forty, so she's either forty or forty-one. Pastor Johanssen must be in his late thirties. But they are getting on; it's time for both of them to wake up."

The sun had set by the time Doc Moore and Ron returned—without Ruth. "It's a break," Doc said. "Kind of a tricky one. They want to keep her overnight. I'll go back in the morning."

Ron shook his head. "I'm kicking myself that we didn't take her to the hospital immediately, but she's stubborn." He'd return the next afternoon to see her, but he had appointments in the morning.

We thanked the Moores and started back. This time, Todd drove—neither Ron nor I objected. The promised rain was with us all the way back. Todd kept his mind on the road. Ron and I were quiet. We had run out of conversation. I didn't know about Ron, but I had also run out of thoughts.

It was ten o'clock when we finally reached home and rushed inside to see if Mom had called back. Hal was still awake and handed me a slip of paper.

"Mom, it's me. Don't say much; just tell me where you are."

Her voice shook, but she gave me the name of a motel on Horizon Drive near the airport. "Todd is with you? He's safe?"

"Yes. Mom, we'll come get you in the morning. Don't say anything more. Grand Valley phones still have a party line, and someone has been very curious about my conversations."

"All right. I'll be waiting. Goodnight, honey." I struggled to hold back the tears.

"She didn't say anything about Dad?"

"I didn't let her say much, in case someone was listening. It's hard to wait longer, but let's hope we get some answers soon."

Todd went upstairs, and I talked briefly with Hal about all that had occurred. He said we could bring Mom back with us. "But I don't know for how long, Meg. You might not be staying here much longer, either. The doctors say Freddy will need a lot of rehabilitation, and they also recommend a special school outside of Denver, if"—Hal's voice broke—"if he makes it, that is."

"Of course he'll make it." Platitudes. What did I know? Touching his arm, I gently said goodnight.

I had settled into bed when I heard a commotion in the hall, followed by a knock at my door. Both Todd and Artie were standing there.

"What's wrong?"

"Todd's room was ransacked."

"Anything missing?"

"Nothing," Todd said. "I gave you most of the money, Meg. Everything else I brought of value is in my pockets. How could someone get into the house?"

Artie shrugged. "It's never locked, and we didn't come home from Grand Junction until late afternoon."

"Someone took an awful chance, though. What were they looking for?" The boys shook their heads. "Artie, the photos? Do you have them?"

"No, Ruth's friend hasn't delivered them yet."

"Contact him in the morning—not by phone, though—and find out if they've been developed. And maybe you should ask him to hold on to them."

"Or at least one copy and the negatives. Dad could lock a set in his safe."

There was nothing more to be done that night. Artie offered to help Todd straighten the room. Before I fell asleep, I had a wisp of memory—something Mom told Todd to take when he left our house. Money and something else. I'd ask Todd in the morning.

Chapter Twenty

"Drive Mom's car carefully," I said. "The roads are a mess, and remember, someone is after us and probably Mom, too."

"I wonder what they were looking for in my room. And why wasn't yours searched?"

I couldn't answer that but recalled my last thought before going to sleep. "Back in Des Plaines, when Mom called, she told you to take money and something else. What else?"

Todd pulled keys from his pocket and jingled them. "Just a few keys from Dad's desk drawer. I put them on this ring and didn't think anything more about them."

"And they've been with you the entire time? What are they for?"

Todd shook his head. "Other than for the car and house, I have no idea. It was so crazy back then I didn't give them another thought."

"They must be important." Clearly, he shouldn't carry them any longer. "Todd, let's stop off and see Ron. It's early, but he'll be in his office. I'll wait in the car. Ask him to lock Dad's keys in a safe place. If someone goes after us today, at least they won't get them."

Todd returned surprisingly fast. "Done," he said, "and Ron said Ruth's ankle has been set and he'll bring her home this afternoon."

"I wonder if she'll be able to teach Monday." I wasn't really concerned about that, but it felt good to think about something commonplace for a change.

"We were planning on talking to the Tuckers today," Todd said. "Maybe I'll go while you're helping Mom settle in at the Gowers'."

"Todd, no—absolutely not. I'm starting to think the two of us together won't be enough."

"Then who else? Ron again?"

"I was thinking of asking Hal, although we'll have to wait another day if he's busy. He works for the Bureau of Mines and might be able to talk with Milt Tucker easier than Ron could." And I needed to call Walt from a Grand Junction pay phone to tell him about the driver of the Buick. I decided not to mention this to Todd.

"Do you think it's safe for Mom in Grand Valley? I know Hal said she could stay with us, but . . ."

"Let's wait and see what Mom has to say." I didn't think it was a good idea, either, but she couldn't stay in Grand Junction; the drive was too far. Perhaps she and Todd could stay at a hotel in Rifle. First, however, we had to find out about Dad.

At the front desk, I asked for Mrs. Shaw's room number. "I'm sorry. No one by that name is registered here."

"What?"

"Let me try, Meg. What about Candace Cramer?"

The desk clerk smiled. "Yes, Miss Cramer is in Room 219."

My clever brother. Cramer was Mom's maiden name. She was being cautious.

"Yes?" was the soft response to our knock on the door.

"It's us, Mom," Todd said. "Open the door."

We heard the security chain slide and the door opened, not quite all the way. Mom quickly pulled us into the room and locked the door again. She gathered Todd into her arms and then me, before bursting out crying.

This tired, gray woman was my mom? I hardly recognized her. "Todd, why are you here? I thought you'd stay with a friend in Des Plaines until I could contact you."

"You never said that, Mom. You told me to get out, so I did." Todd told her about finding the hotel phone number and driving to Washington. She was as horrified as I about his long, dangerous drive. She wouldn't tell us anything until we got her up to date on everything that had happened to us.

"And the keys?" she asked.

Todd admitted their importance hadn't registered with him until that morning and that he had removed them from his key chain right before we left Grand Valley.

"Where are they now?"

"Locked up in the office safe of a good friend," I said. "We were afraid to have them with us in case someone succeeded in forcing us off the road. Are the keys what this is about?"

"I don't know, but I'm afraid they might be. Sit down. I've got a lot to tell you."

"Like where Dad is?"

"I don't know the answer to that. But I will tell you what I do know."

First, Todd loaded up on vending machine snacks and drinks for all of us. The normality of Todd thinking about food seemed to help Mom relax a little. Much of her anguish had come from worrying about Todd.

"I hardly know where to begin," she said.

"Start with the morning I woke up, and you weren't there." Todd sounded angry now, and I couldn't blame him.

"Not even a note, Mom? Todd was scared." He nodded, not denying it.

Mom gave a deep sigh. "I'll admit I've made a lot of mistakes. Dad went to testify on behalf of the environmentalists who were against

Project Rulison. He thought it was a losing fight, but he felt he had to at least try."

Well, that was good. Finally, we knew for sure which side he was on. I grabbed a handful of pretzels and munched, deciding not to comment on Mom's mistakes.

"You didn't want Meg to come to Grand Valley, Mom. Why not?"

"Because of the way she was offered the job. It didn't make sense. I thought the Tuckers might be behind it."

"They were," I said, my speech garbled, "or at least Caroline Tucker was. She's on the school board. But what did anyone have to gain from my being here?"

"Nothing really, but Milton Tucker is an odd, twisted man, and his wife always thinks everyone has it better than she has. That's probably true, but she married him."

"He calls Dad a thief," I said. "Why?"

"It's because of the uranium. Both men made a fair amount of money. This was in the early fifties before the Atomic Energy Commission took over, and your father started working for them and the Bureau of Mines. He invested his money wisely and watched it grow, but Milt didn't. He lost everything but got it into his head that Chet owed him a share of what he had. That wasn't true, but truth and Milt never had much to do with each other."

"Why did we leave Colorado so suddenly?"

"And why did Dad think it was okay for Meg to come here?"

"Let's go back to Todd's first question. I'll answer everything, but it might help if we aren't all over the place."

Todd and I kept quiet.

Apparently, Mom had received a phone call that morning, before Todd awoke, saying if she didn't stop Dad, he would not be alive to testify. "Your father left his hotel phone number for me. I called, but he wasn't there. I guess I went a little crazy; at least, I wasn't thinking straight. I called a cab, grabbed my purse, and was in Washington before noon."

"You didn't leave Todd a note."

"No, I thought I'd call him later."

"You did," Todd said, "only it was much later."

"Did you find Dad?"

"Yes, mid-afternoon. I stayed in the hotel room and waited for him. I would have called, Todd, but I didn't think you'd be home. You usually aren't."

That was true.

"Finally Chet came, just to freshen up before going back to court. He said his affidavit would be taken as soon as he arrived. He would not be testifying, but his statement would be read there—if the court actually agreed to meet. Afterwards, we would fly home together. Then he said something that scared me."

"What?"

Mom almost whispered the words. "That if anything happened to him, above all, to guard his keys. That was the last time I saw him." She tried to call Todd then, but the line was busy. Just as she was about to try again, her phone rang. "Another threatening phone call—only this time, you were threatened, Todd." The unknown voice—a man's—had said, "Go home and get all of your husband's documents, or you'll never see your son or husband."

Mom started to cry again. "I tried to find your father. I contacted a few people he knew in Washington—business associates. One of them said Chet never reached the courthouse. Then I made another attempt to reach Todd, and he finally answered."

"And you told me to take the money and Dad's keys and get out." Todd looked at me. "She was in a state of panic, Meggy."

That had always been the way. I was Dad's child, and Todd was Mom's. He was defending her as usual. "What are the keys for, Mom?" I asked. "Someone seems willing to kill to get them."

"I'm not sure. Normal things, but one probably opens a safety deposit box. He doesn't keep any important documents in the house."

No doubt the AEC wanted whatever was in the box. "What did you do then, Mom?"

"I left a message for your father at the desk and told the concierge not to give out information about us to anyone."

"Which ended up including Todd, Libby, and me."

"What?"

"I didn't know what happened. I had Libby go into the house. She found the Washington phone number and gave it to me, but I couldn't get any information from the Hay-Adams."

"Oh, no . . ."

"It's okay, Mom," Todd said, "you didn't know, and they wouldn't have been able to help Meggy anyway. What information could they give—our address and phone number in Des Plaines?"

Well, that was true. "What did you do next?"

"I went home. Then I checked with Todd's friends. None of them had seen him. Then I went to my sister's house and hoped Todd would think to call there. Finally, I came here."

Time went by while she did nothing but wait with her sister in Chicago. She certainly never called me. But I held my tongue. Blame wouldn't accomplish anything. I almost didn't care about answers to the other questions—unless they would help find Dad. He was all that mattered now.

"Maybe instead of more questions, we should start back to Grand Valley, but I need to make a few phone calls first." I called Hal. "We'll be coming home as soon as we stop off at the hospital. Then I wonder if you'll go somewhere with us. We need to ask someone a few questions, and it might be easier with you there. I shouldn't say more over the phone."

"I understand," he said.

After he hung up, I dialed another number. "Walt Jeffreys." Walt began to cough.

"It's Meg. Are you sick?"

He cleared his throat. "Oh, it's nothing. I'm glad you called."

"Listen carefully. I need you to do something important. Do you have any photos of the men who talked to all of us at the GV hall? The people from the Commission?"

"Yes, I have some group shots."

"Good. Could you bring them to Grand Valley tonight?"

"Tonight? I couldn't possibly. Maybe in a few days . . ."

"No, Walt, it needs to be tonight. I need to look at those pictures. At least one of those men is trying to kill my family."

"You're kidding . . ."

"Do I sound like I am? Tonight, Walt, or we're finished before we've even begun. Unless you come, I will assume you're one of them."

"I'll be there. Meg, are you in danger?"

"Yes, and so are my mother, father, and brother. Come tonight." I hung up.

Mom stared at me. "You've changed," she said.

I had, and so had Todd, but clearly my mother hadn't—at least not enough to be much help. I made a decision, checked the phone book, and dialed the Old Midland. I booked a room for two, starting tomorrow night, and gave my mother's maiden name. "I'm not sure exactly how long they'll be staying," I said. "At least two nights."

"Meg," Todd protested. I stopped him with a look.

"Mom, let's get you checked out of here, and then see how Freddy is doing."

"You asked Mr. Gower to go with us to question someone?" Mom said.

"The Tuckers. I don't think we can put it off any longer. It may help that you're with us. Todd and I had already decided to ask Hal."

"Oh, I don't know if that's such a good idea."

Todd patted her hand. "We need to do this, Mom. All these secrets aren't keeping Dad safe. Milt Tucker won't try anything with Hal there." She nodded, but I could tell she was frightened about confronting him.

Todd wasn't pleased that both he and Mom would be leaving Grand Valley the next day. I tried to explain. "The Gowers are packing for Denver; we shouldn't take advantage of their hospitality. You'll be safer in Rifle, and it's only a short drive from the Gowers' house. The Moores will be pleased to see Mom, and it's important to be able to make private phone calls. Think of Rifle as Command Central." Todd perked up at those words. Command Central was just the thing to bring out the kid in him.

We met Ethel in the visiting area on Freddy's floor. She and I embraced like the dearest of long lost friends. "How is he doing?" I asked, after I introduced her to Mom.

"They're ready to move him to Denver by helicopter, but he refuses to go in one."

"Understandable," I said, "but isn't it wonderful he's strong enough to care about anything?"

She gave me a shaky smile. "You're right about that."

"Could Meg and I talk to him about it?" Todd asked. "I had a friend once—well, he was a lot like Freddy."

Jimmy. I'd forgotten about the greatest loss in Todd's life. Jimmy had been Todd's best friend, although they didn't attend the same school. Jimmy had Down Syndrome more severely than Freddy. Todd had met him in a park playground, and they had become firm friends. Sadly, Jimmy had died when he was only thirteen.

"Todd would be a good person to talk to Freddy," Mom said.

Ethel gave permission, so we walked toward Freddy's room. "He is much more advanced than Jimmy," I said, "and he's sixteen-years-old already."

Considering all Freddy had been through, he looked better than I expected. Pale, thinner, and without his usual joyfulness, he looked more his age. He gestured toward his water glass and took a sip once I handed it to him. "Meg," he said in a hoarse voice, "you've come to see me."

"I have, Freddy, and I brought my brother. This is Todd."

Todd sat next to him and started talking about interesting cars he had seen on his drive west. It seemed an odd conversation to me, but I guessed Todd knew what he was doing. Freddy's natural smile returned, and I could tell he felt comfortable with Todd.

"And the trains—wow! I saw so many trains. And when I drove across the Prairie states, I could see the whole train, all stretched out, from the engine to the caboose. Back home, buildings would be in the way."

"And the mountains out here," I said. "You never see a whole train at once in Grand Valley." Where was Todd going with this?

"I saw some airplanes, too. Big ones and little ones, and even a few helicopters."

Freddy reacted. "I hate helicopters," he said. "The helicopter shot Freddy."

"I heard about that," Todd said. "It was a terrible thing to do. But Freddy, you know there are good people and bad people, right?"

Freddy took another sip of water before nodding.

"Well, it's the same with cars. A bad car tried to drive Meg and me off the road, but that doesn't mean all cars are bad. We were in Pastor Johanssen's car, and his car is very good."

You could almost see Freddy's brain at work. "Helicopters?"

"That's right, although a person shot you, not the helicopter. There are bad helicopters and good ones. The hospital only has good ones. The doctors want a good helicopter to take you and your family to a special hospital in Denver so you can get better even faster."

"A good one would be okay," Freddy said, and closed his eyes. We left the room quietly.

"You're a genius," I said. Todd's eyes were brimming with tears. He grieved still for his friend.

Back in the waiting room, we told Ethel what had happened, and she rushed to call Hal with the good news. A new visitor had arrived. Mr. Owens. Clearly, Mr. Owens had problems of his own.

"I just heard about Ruth," he said. "I don't think we'll be able to resume classes on Monday, Miss Shaw—Meg."

This would not be bad news for me. Still—"I'm sure Carrie, Effie, and I can handle the children," I said.

"That's the other problem. Carrie's gone. She quit. Her mother was so rattled by the test the family upped and moved away."

"We've all got a lot going on," I said. "It might be a good plan to wait until Wednesday or even another week." Carrie and I could handle things, but Effie? I wasn't so sure.

"I think you're right," Mr. Owens said. "Effie will conduct a little art and music class to help out working parents, and the ladies at the church might be willing to take a few older children into their new play group." He sighed. "We'll have to end classes later in May, but this will give me more time to adjust teaching schedules again."

And me more time to find Dad.

Chapter Twenty-One

"I DIDN'T DO NUTHIN'." MILT Tucker glared at us.

Hal just grinned at him. "Good afternoon to you, too, Milt."

Caroline Tucker came up behind him. "What are you people doing here?"

"Well now, Caroline," Hal drawled, "that's not very friendly for someone in your position. Why don't you let us in, and we'll just sit a spell and talk?"

I doubt if the Tuckers would have let us in the house if Hal hadn't come. Both of them seemed startled to see Mom. At least there was something they didn't already know. Ungraciously, Caroline half-gestured to the living room, where we sat, waiting for someone to speak. "Mom?" I prompted.

She nodded. She was not confrontational; this was hard for her. "Milt, where is my husband?"

"What are you talking about? Haven't seen him in years—not since you left like thieves in the night."

"Which is what you go around saying to anyone who'll listen to your nonsense," Hal said.

"Ain't nonsense. Just want what's comin' to me."

"And what might that be, Mr. Tucker?"

"Don't have to answer some hippy kid."

"This hippy kid is my son, Todd Shaw," Mom said, "and someone is trying to kill him."

"And me," I added. "Is that why you brought me out here, Mrs. Tucker, or was it because Dad was sure to follow and you could get at him?"

"Why, I'll sue." Mrs. Tucker turned bright red, not a good look with her pink and orange dress. "You can't go around talking lies like that."

"Maybe we'll counter-sue," Todd said, "because of the lies you're spreading about Dad."

Hal stopped the back-and-forth jabs. "Let's talk about your claim that Charles Shaw is a thief. Seems to me you need some evidence."

"I had more money coming to me from the uranium I found, that's all I know."

"That's ridiculous, Milt Tucker, and you know it." Finally, Mom was getting mad. "The AEC made the decision how much money was due to each of you. Neither you nor Chet had anything to say about it. My husband made shrewd investments with his share, while you . . ."

"Drank it up," Caroline finished softly. "I didn't know it was the AEC's doing."

"Why did you want me to teach here, Mrs. Tucker?"

"Wasn't me," she said. "It was the whole school board. That's all I'm saying."

It appeared that was all either of them would say. Before we left, I tried again. It might not have been wise, but I was certain the Tuckers were lying, and I needed to give them something to think about.

"Someone tried to run us off the road," I said. "Todd, Ruth Arnold, Pastor Johanssen, and I were nearly killed. But I recognized the driver, and I can identify him. We're going to learn the truth. You might consider how much better it will be for you if we don't have to learn the hard way." I thought I'd shocked the Tuckers, but I couldn't tell for sure.

"Do you think that was smart?" Mom asked, as we returned to the car.

"Maybe not," I said, "but they were lying, and I didn't want things to end the way they were going to."

"I agree," Todd said. "Too many secrets."

"I forgot to ask whether or not they were listening to my phone calls."

"Doesn't matter, Meg. They wouldn't admit it." Todd was right, of course.

My spirits lifted at a sight outside of Ruth's house. There was Ron, helping her leave his car. Ruth seemed to be an expert already at managing her crutches. Hal pulled to a stop, and I rolled down my window. "I'll come see you later," I promised. I'd missed Ruth's steady good sense. We should have waited until she could have helped question the Tuckers.

When we arrived at the Gowers', we introduced Mom to Hal and Artie, who offered Freddy's room to Todd—"I heard you were able to talk Freddy into taking the helicopter ride. Thanks."—and added that he'd fix up the guest room for Mom.

After a quick supper, I walked over to Ruth's, leaving strict instructions I was to be called there if Walt showed up.

"Don't fuss, I'm fine," Ruth insisted, as I busied myself in her kitchen. "You're fixing me tea and toast? I broke my ankle, not my stomach."

I got her caught up on everything—Freddy's progress, Carrie leaving Grand Valley, Mom's story, and our unproductive meeting with the Tuckers. "I don't know if I should have mentioned the driver of the Buick," I said.

"You gave them fair warning to tell what they know, but you also put them on guard. Time will tell if you did the right thing. Now it's my turn."

Ruth told me to open an envelope on the counter. "The photos!" I looked through them quickly. Most were too fuzzy to make out much, but we got lucky. The ones of the men in the helicopter were clear, especially that of the shooter. "We got him!"

"Do you recognize him, Meg?"

"No, but someone will. We've got extra prints and the negatives—right?"

"Absolutely. Someone is bound to try to suppress them."

The phone rang. "He's here."

That's all Todd needed to say. I tried to make sure Ruth had everything she needed, but she shooed me out the door. "Don't fuss. Ron will be over later to check on me. I told him it wasn't necessary, but . . ." Hard to believe, but Ruth actually blushed. "Take the photos with you, and be careful."

I could hear Walt's hacking cough from the front door. He, Todd, and Hal were waiting for me in the study. Walt had a folder with him. He seemed disturbed. Both Todd and Hal must have been giving him a hard time.

"What's this about, Meg?"

"May I see the photos, Walt?"

I looked carefully at a group shot of AEC members. Of course, I had seen all ten at the meeting, but other than Walt, three looked familiar from other times. I was certain of one.

"Todd, ask Artie to come down. I've got the photos he and I took."

"You kept some from me?"

"I had my reasons."

Todd returned, accompanied by Artie. "You've got the photos, Meg? Let me see them."

"In a minute." I returned to Walt's collection. "This is the man who tried to drive us off the road." I pointed to the only man with a mustache and a slight beard. He was taller and thinner than the others.

"Why that's . . ." Walt began to cough. I couldn't tell if it was intentional.

"I know his name," Hal said. "This is almost unbelievable."

"It is unbelievable," Walt said.

"I said 'almost.' What are the other photos, Meg?"

"Ones Artie and I took at Ground Zero. Ruth had someone develop them, but I won't say who. Walt, you need to know we have duplicates and the negatives." I pulled one out and showed it to Artie. Then I handed it to Hal. "This is the man who shot Freddy."

Neither Walt nor Hal could deny what they saw. Wildly, without thinking, I had managed to capture the shooter still holding his gun and Freddy looking back at him as if he couldn't believe what had occurred. I could tell both of them knew the gunman's identity.

"And just what are you going to do with this information, Walt?" Hal was livid.

"I'm not sure. After all, they were trespassing."

I couldn't believe my ears. "And trespassers—children—deserve to be shot? Is that what you believe, Walt? Should Ruth, Artie, and I be shot, too?"

"No, of course not. It's just that . . ."

"That's what they're going to say," Hal said. "The Commission, the government, anyone who doesn't want the truth to come out. But my son was nearly killed, Walt, and he's got a long recovery ahead of him. We must get to the bottom of this."

Walt nodded, unhappily.

I handed him the package of photos and looked at one of the group shots again. "I can't be certain, but this is the man I saw talking to my father near the viewing site."

"It was awfully far away," Artie said.

"Yes, I know, but I think it was him."

"Nice associates you've got, Mr. Jeffreys." Todd couldn't have made his disapproval of Walt much clearer.

Nothing more could be done that night. Walt would bed down on a couch in the study since all of the bedrooms were taken. He would return to Denver in the morning and show members of the Commission the photos.

"You may need to go to Washington," Hal said. "We don't have any proof against Ben and Lawrence, but the authorities can at least hold Eric for shooting a civilian."

Walt did not seem pleased that Hal had given names, but I thought Hal now agreed with Todd. The time for secrets was over. Artie, Todd, and Hal left the study, but I lingered behind.

"Meg?" Walt held out his arms to me.

"Just find my father."

"This could ruin me, you know."

"I guess that's a risk you'll have to take."

He began to cough again, but I had no sympathy for him. "Better see someone about that cough, Walt."

Chapter Twenty-Two

WALT WAS GONE WHEN I awoke. At my insistence, Mom and Todd were soon on their way to the Old Midland. Mom was in too much of a daze to care where she went, but Todd protested. "I don't see why this is necessary, Meg."

I gave a great sigh but tried again. "Hal and Artie are busy," I said. "I'll help them, but I think three Shaws would be in the way. Besides, you'll be safer in Rifle. Mom can reconnect with the Moores, and your hotel room won't have a party line." Todd wasn't convinced, but left—finally.

Hal put me in charge of packing up the kitchen, although most of their possessions would go into storage in Rifle until plans were more definite. "I made some calls," he said. "There's a facility outside of Denver in a community called Rocky Flats. I'll be able to get work there and rent a furnished house. It's close to the hospital where Freddy needs to go, and there's a high school for Artie."

"High school?"

Hal smiled. "Yes, he told me about your conversation. I can't thank you enough. Ethel called the new school and explained the circumstances. They're going to let Artie take some tests."

"He should do just fine."

Hal left, so I finished packing the pots and pans before going to Artie's room. "Need any help?" I asked.

"No, I'm okay. It seems funny to be leaving here."

"But you didn't want to come."

"I know. That seems funny now, too."

"I'll miss you," I said.

He nodded. "But it's not that far away, and . . ."

". . . they're building a new highway." We both laughed.

"Dad is selling the place. Some people want to remodel it for a hotel. Odd time to be doing that, but who cares? Where will you go, Meg?"

"Until I find out about my father, I can't even think about it."

"Wait—I hear someone calling. What?" he shouted.

"It's me—Todd."

I dashed downstairs. "What are you doing here? Where's Mom?"

"With Mrs. Moore. Milt Tucker had a heart attack. Doc rushed out there, but he thought you should know about it, so I drove out, too. Milt was taken by helicopter to Denver, but Doc doesn't think he's going to make it. Meg, I think we should go see Mrs. Tucker right now."

"Caroline didn't go with them?"

Todd shook his head. "Maybe she'll be rattled enough to tell us something. Pastor Johanssen is going with us as soon as his service is over. Ruth should, too, if she's up to it."

Todd went over to the church to wait for Ron, and I went to Ruth's. Both of us got into the car when they came for us.

Ron was not pleased. "You shouldn't be going anywhere on that leg, Ruth. Go back inside."

"Nope, so stop fussing. I'm not sure seeing Caroline is a good idea, but since you insist upon it, I'm going, too. You need me."

Ruth was right. We did.

Caroline opened the door right away. "I've been expecting you," she said quietly.

"How is Milt doing?" Ruth asked.

"He's alive, but the doctors don't think for much longer. I'm not sure what to wish for. I can guess why you're here." Caroline led us to the living room, where she opened a secretary drawer and pulled out some papers. "I'm truly sorry this all happened."

I looked through the papers and then handed them over to Ron and Ruth. "It's kind of an informal contract," I said to Todd. "It looks as if Mr. Tucker was paid money to kidnap Dad."

"Oh, not actually kidnap," Caroline protested. "Milt was just supposed to get him out of the way for a while until they could get what they wanted." *They* was the Atomic Energy Commission of the United States.

"Sounds to me like the very definition of kidnapping, Caroline," Ruth said.

"Milt and I never meant to hurt anyone," she whined, "but we needed the money."

"What was your part in this, Caroline?" Ron asked, as soon as he was through studying the papers. "It doesn't say."

"I agreed to encourage the school board to hire Miss Shaw—I was told what university she was attending—and once she was here, I agreed to keep track of whatever she did in Grand Valley."

"And you did this how? By listening in on my phone conversations?"

Caroline nodded but didn't say anything.

Todd grabbed the papers. "There's nothing here about where my father is now. Do you know?"

Caroline remained silent.

"Please, Mrs. Tucker," I begged. "We must find him."

"It will go better for you, Caroline, if you tell us everything," Ruth added.

Caroline shrugged. "I guess I don't have anything more to lose." She opened another drawer and took out a torn, ancient-looking survey map. She handed it to Ron, who spread it out on the coffee table.

"Where is this?" he asked.

"I'm not entirely sure," Caroline said, "but I think it likely Milt and another man took Chet here," and she pointed to a spot on the map.

"Where is that?" Todd asked.

"Oh, no!" I spoke in a voice I didn't recognize. "Dad has a map like that. It's one of the shale mines at Anvil Points. They're all boarded up now."

"Do you mean to tell me, Caroline Tucker, that Chet Shaw has been a prisoner in an abandoned mine for four days?" Ruth shook with rage.

Caroline began to whimper. "I don't know if it's been that long."

"You better start praying it hasn't been," Ron said. "In fact, you better start praying, period."

We took the papers and map and left Caroline to her prayers. Ron drove us back to the Gowers', and then he and Hal left immediately to round up all the men they could. Todd and Artie put together some first aid supplies while Ruth fretted that she would not be allowed to join the rescue mission, even though she knew that physically she couldn't handle it.

Artie had news. "Doc Moore called. Milt Tucker passed away. And Walt Jeffreys called, too. He's in Washington. He doesn't know if they'll make the charges stick, but they are holding the three men for questioning."

"That's good," I said. "At least we don't have to worry about bumping into them tonight."

Ruth decided to stay at the Gowers' house and receive phone calls. "And I'll call one of Caroline's friends to go be with her. She's going to need someone." We all agreed it would be a mistake to contact Mom. We would let her know as soon as something was definite.

Todd drove Mom's car. I noticed that Dad's keys were back on the key chain in the ignition. I supposed it no longer mattered. Artie climbed into the back seat, and I sat next to Todd. Ron and Hal were riding in a jeep with some men I didn't know. Another jeep followed, driven by Ray Owens, and our car brought up the rear. We'd transfer the first aid supplies to a jeep once we got to Anvil Points. It would not be safe to drive our car up the narrow road to the mine. It wouldn't be safe for the jeeps, either, if they didn't complete the trip before nightfall.

There was less than an hour of daylight left when we reached Anvil Points. The men would not allow Artie, Todd, or me to complete the last trek. "But he's our father!" Todd protested. They agreed then to include Todd. Perhaps it would help Dad to hear a voice he recognized, but Artie and I were to remain behind in the car.

"I'm strong," Artie said, as soon as the jeeps started up the high narrow trail. "I could help."

"Yes, you could, but I'm not sure about me. And Artie, I don't think I could bear waiting alone."

My words made him feel a little better. We talked some—about his experiences in Denver and his mixed emotions about returning there. I told him about being a child right here and about my home in Des Plaines. The sun went down. We ran out of chatter and became quiet in the darkness, each with our own miserable thoughts.

The wait seemed endless, but it was just under two hours when I saw lights moving slowly down a trail never meant for night travel. I nudged Artie, who had fallen asleep. "They're back. Wake up."

We stood next to the car and followed the jeeps with our eyes, as they made their way around each precarious turn. The first jeep stopped next to us; the second kept on going. Hal came over and took my hands in his. "We found him, Meg. Barely conscious, but he's alive. Ron and Todd are taking him to the hospital in Rifle. He had some food and a few blankets, but no light, and it was very cold."

Artie got into the jeep with his father. "Call when you know something, Meg. I hope your dad is okay."

He's just got to be, I thought. Energized, now that there was something definite to do, I drove the eight miles to Rifle—first to the Moores' to pick up Mom, and then to the hospital.

Chapter Twenty-Three

Dad was malnourished, dehydrated, and dangerously close to hypothermia, but he gave us a wan smile and held out his hand to Mom, who looked almost as ill as he. "To think that you found me, and you're all here. Or am I hallucinating?"

Todd grinned. "No, it's us, Dad. Would you like me to pinch you?"

"I knew I saw you at the site," I said.

"I got a telegram, but it was a trap. I'll tell you more later . . . Some things . . ." Dad's eyes started to close. "We'll all have stories to tell . . ." I wondered if some of the stories might never be told.

A nurse shooed us out, so we returned to the Old Midland. I could have booked another room. We would be crowded. But Mom, Todd, and I didn't even check with each other. We knew we needed to stay together that night.

Dad was awake the next morning when we arrived at the hospital, but we could tell he wasn't ready for questions. Doc Moore had visited already and told Dad he would remain there at least until the end of the week. Perhaps he, Mom, and Todd would be able to drive home over the weekend. I had until then to decide if I would be one of the passengers.

We returned to the Old Midland, where I booked a room of my own and slept the entire day. We joined the Moores for dinner at the hotel, and then Todd drove me back to Grand Valley, where I would continue to help the Gowers pack and wait for Dad to get better. When I arrived, I learned that Ethel and Freddy had already made the helicopter trip to Denver. The ride had been hard on Freddy, but he remained in stable condition.

The greatest pleasure I had that week was the feeling, finally, of normality—or at least of not being in danger. I could make a phone call without wondering who might be listening. Yes, I was worried about what was happening with Walt and if the men who had endangered us would be brought to justice, and I still had questions for my parents. For the moment, though, I was content with a timeout from danger, and the extended break from teaching was also welcome.

On Wednesday, a whole week after the disastrous test, with many blushes and stutters, Ruth told me her news. She and Ron were engaged. "After knowing each other for such a long time, we finally figured out how we felt," she said. I gave her a hug and proudly accepted her request to be a bridesmaid. "Right after school is out in May." If I ended up going back to Des Plaines, I would still return for the wedding.

Whether to stay or not was the key decision facing me. If I remained, I needed to find another place to live. Hal and Artie were leaving in another week. I hadn't enjoyed my few teaching days, but the conditions had been strange, and I hadn't given it much of a chance. Ruth thought I should stay, but her little house wasn't large enough to share, and she'd be moving in with Ron as soon as they married. She supposed I could bunk on her couch until I figured out what to do.

Ron mentioned that Caroline Tucker was leaving Grand Valley to live with her sister in Durango. "You should go see her, Meg, and offer forgiveness—for her sake and for your own."

"No, Ron," I said. "Not yet and perhaps never. We wouldn't have learned the truth if Milt hadn't had a heart attack, and Dad would have died. She is lucky we're not bringing charges against her." Ron wisely said nothing.

Dad was released on Saturday. He, Mom, and Todd would start the long trip home the next morning. He was too weak to drive, but Mom and Todd would take turns. I finally made my decision. I would go to Ruth's on Monday, the same day classes resumed.

While we were waiting for Dad, Mom, and Todd to come to Grand Valley to say goodbye, Hal received a phone call from Walt, saying he was coming, too. Artie and I dashed over to Hannah's Sandwich to buy supplies for lunch. Practically everything the Gowers owned was packed. Fortunately, we bought a lot, because the Moores, Ruth, and Ron showed up as well. They all wanted to meet Dad.

Everyone took a great liking to him, especially Hal. I could tell he planned to spirit Dad into his study the minute lunch was over. Walt was late, but that was for the best. No one would be comfortable around him. The Moores and Ron left right after coffee and dessert, and Artie went to his room. Todd started to follow him but changed his mind and followed Hal and Dad into the study.

"Todd is at that in-between stage," Mom said. "He's not sure what world he belongs in." She, Ruth, and I had sat down in the kitchen for one more cup of coffee when Walt arrived.

"Sorry I'm so late," he said. Right away, he asked to meet Dad.

Mom frowned. "For a few minutes. We need to get back to Rifle."

I accompanied Walt into Hal's study. Walt seemed nervous. Not surprising, under the circumstances.

After introductions, Hal asked about the three men in Washington. "It doesn't look good," Walt said. "From what I heard, they didn't deny anything, but they weren't forthcoming with the truth, either. But I don't believe they're a threat now."

"That's pretty much what I expected," Hal said. "The government will suppress it. My guess is they'll be assigned somewhere else—far away from here. I'll touch base with you later, Walt. I promised to take Ruth home. Pleasure meeting you, Chet."

As soon as Hal left, Walt started to talk about Dad's writings. It felt like small talk, and I could tell Dad was becoming tired. Then Todd pulled the car keys from his pocket. "The forecast is more rain," Todd said. "We should go."

Walt was staring at Todd. No, he was staring at Todd's key chain. "I'm afraid, Todd, that I must take that key—the small one to the safety deposit box."

"Walt?"

"Stay out of it, Meg." Walt held out his hand. "Todd?"

"No. That's not going to happen. What are you up to, anyway?"

"I'm afraid it's obvious," Dad said. "It was nice meeting you, Mr. Jeffreys, but my family and I are leaving now."

"Not with that key, you're not." Walt pulled a small gun from his pocket and pointed it at us. "I'm very sorry. You'll never know how sorry, but I am under orders to get that key, no matter what happens."

Even shooting us? I wondered.

Dad nodded. "It appears I was correct that our home and hotel phones were tapped. My trap worked, and I caught a rat. Well, no matter. Let me have the keys, Todd."

Todd placed the key ring in Dad's hand, and Dad took inventory. "Let's see: car key, house key, garage key, key to my locker at the gym, and this one—the one you'd kill to have." He removed it from the key ring. "You'll find it fits a safety deposit box at the Des Plaines First National Bank. Number #546. You might want to write that down after you put your gun away. Normally, the bank won't let just anyone into their vaults, but it appears you aren't just anyone." He handed the key to Walt.

"Dad, don't," Todd pleaded.

Dad ignored him. "Just be sure to mail it back to me once you, or whoever controls you, goes through the papers, and be sure to put everything back neatly. They won't mean anything to you, but they are important to my family."

"But . . ." Walt started.

"There are no documents, Mr. Jeffreys, other than the ones filed up here"—Dad pointed to his head—"and you may not have those. In the box, you'll find a marriage certificate, four birth certificates, and the deeds to our cars and house. You've been given some bad information. Put your gun away. Your people have nothing to fear from me. Do your worst to me, but I will keep my family safe."

Slowly, Walt returned the gun to his pocket. "Meg?"

"You knew who I was all along, Walt. You were using me to get to my father."

"Only at first."

I turned my back on him and walked out of the room.

"Meg, wait . . ."

I returned to teaching on Monday. I had a lot to learn, but I was willing to make the effort. After school, I packed my suitcase and lugged it over to a once-gray house with paint hanging off its sides in great peels. Carefully, I climbed the wooden stairs of the rickety front porch that lacked a railing, and knocked on the door.

"Meggy?"

"You need a paying boarder, Loreen, and I need a place to live."

Epilogue

"And that's my story," Aunt Meg concluded. She had been talking for hours while I raptly listened.

"But that couldn't be all. What happened next?"

"Next? Why I lived happily ever after with your Grandma Loreen—until she retired and moved to California."

"No, please, Aunt Meg, don't end it there. You've left so much unanswered."

She seemed depleted and no longer interested. "What must you know today that is so urgent?"

"Please?"

"Very well, but only a few questions."

I wasn't sure where to start? Nothing was urgent—just interesting. "Did you stay in Grand Valley?"

"Oh, yes, although it's called Parachute now. I taught school for many years—even became principal when Ray retired—and helped your grandma raise Jana and your aunt and uncle. When Loreen moved, I bought the little house Ruth used to own. Dear Loreen. I can't believe she's gone. I miss her every day."

Tears came into Aunt Meg's eyes. If I didn't change the subject, I would lose her. "Were there more nuclear tests?"

"Just one—Rio Blanco. That one was in Rifle, with the same results as Project Rulison."

"Was Walt there?"

"Yes, he was still a believer back then. Funny, that's when I realized he wouldn't be around much longer . . ." her voice drifted off.

I knew Aunt Meg's parents were dead and her brother and his family lived in Illinois. "What about the others? What happened to Ethel and Hal, Artie and Freddy, Ron and Ruth?"

Aunt Meg sighed. "Ethel, Hal, and Freddy died a long time ago. Moving to Rocky Flats was not such a good idea after all. Ron and Ruth retired to Hawaii in the last town where Ron served as pastor. Dear Artie is a music professor at Mesa University in Grand Junction. I'm so very proud of him." Her eyes started to close.

"Did you ever find out why you left Anvil Points so suddenly?" I was not ready to let her go.

"I did." Aunt Meg's eyes popped open again, and for a moment they flashed the dynamic person she used to be. "My father told me the full story shortly before he died. They paid him off. That's why we left so abruptly. The government paid him a great deal of money to leave immediately and to keep quiet about his findings. And between Milt Tucker's nastiness and the knowledge that Anvil Points was about to close anyway . . ." She shrugged. "So he took the money. Later, he regretted it and started speaking out—until they came after us. Then he stayed quiet for the rest of his life."

"Your dad took a bribe?" I'm sure I sounded indignant.

"Years earlier, I would have been furious, but I've learned that none of us is perfect. When Dad died, his lawyer gave me the documents he'd been keeping safe all that time. They did exist—proof that the natural gas from atomic testing would always be too radioactive to be safe. He also warned of the dangers uranium tailings would bring to the people of Grand Junction."

I'd read about the great number of citizens with leukemia and other cancers because they had built the foundations of their homes with toxic material the government had originally declared harmless. The cleanup had been going on for some years then, and Chet Shaw had been aware of the danger since the early 60s.

Aunt Meg must have guessed what I was thinking. "It would have done him no good, dear. The uranium and the testing meant money and power to too many important people. They would have killed him and his whole family before they let him release those documents. Shortly after I received them, the hit and run accident occurred that left me in this wheelchair. I got the message."

"It wasn't an accident?" I was horrified.

She shook her head. "There is no proof, so I won't discuss it. But now, please go. I'm really very tired."

"Just one more thing. What about Walt?"

"He died, of course. That's what his coughing meant. Lung cancer. He breathed in poison for too long."

"And you never married. Was he the love of your life?"

Aunt Meg chuckled. "By all means, make me the heroine of your little romance. If he was the 'love of my life,' that love certainly never progressed very far. Truth is, I never met anyone I wanted to marry. I've had a fine full life, my dear, with a career that satisfied me, a family I loved, and friendships that endured. And just think, you—Jana's own daughter— coming all this way to visit me. Now, would you pass me that afghan, please? I think I'll take a little nap right here."

"But Aunt Meg, what about Tim?"

"I can't decide for you. Use your brain and warm heart to figure it out. You'll find a way, Susan. Whether or not it's the right way, only time will tell."

"But do you ever wish you and Walt . . ."

"Sometimes," she whispered. "Sometimes when it's very late at night, and I'm all alone . . . Sometimes I do."

Aunt Meg closed her eyes. I covered her gently with the lilac and pink afghan my Aunt Ellen had crocheted so many years ago, and quietly left the room.

Author's Note:

The Real Story of Project Rulison

YES, THERE REALLY WAS A Project Rulison. It was one of a series of nuclear tests to determine if natural gas could be removed easily and economically from deep inside the earth. The Atomic Energy Commission and several oil companies' aims were peaceful. Indeed, Project Rulison was part of a larger program called Operation Plowshare.

On September 10, 1969, a 40-kiloton atomic bomb was detonated underground in the rural community of Rulison, Colorado—about 8 miles southeast of Grand Valley (now called Parachute).

Was the test successful? In a way it was. Large amounts of natural gas were released. However, this gas was determined too radioactive for safe use, and the public outrage after the test brought the project eventually to a close. The final test using an atomic bomb was Project Rio Blanco, in nearby Rifle, May 17, 1973.

You may be asking—Why have I never heard of this before? Indeed, that is a very good question.

While Grand Valley did sustain damage, and several people, who had sneaked out to "bare witness," were stopped at gunpoint and whisked away by helicopter, the extent of the disaster is exaggerated in this work of fiction. Today, Parachute is a vibrant community, where the majority of the residents are too young to remember what happened in their very own backyard.

Uranium Tailings

The references to the problems resulting from uranium tailings in Grand Junction, once known as the "most radioactive town in America," were not exaggerated. During the 1950s and 60s, especially, contractors would haul the tailings from uranium mills to use for fill and to mix with cement. Without knowing the risks, people used this radioactive material to build homes, schools, hospitals, and many other buildings. Some of the contractors acted out of ignorance, but not all of them. While tighter regulations and cleanup began in the 70s and 80s, the problem remains to this day. Also, some of the former standards are no longer considered sufficient. Did people die? They did. Radon gas was created by the tailings. Inhaling radon is the second leading cause of lung cancer.

Rocky Flats

Toward the end of *It's Perfectly Safe . . .,* Hal mentions his new job in Rocky Flats, a community outside of Denver, and later, Aunt Meg infers to her young visitor that moving to Rocky Flats was not a good idea. Hal's job, if he were not a fictitious character, of course, would have been in a plant that produced nuclear bomb components. He would have been involved in the manufacturing of plutonium triggers. The contamination of the water, land, and air due to plutonium accidents in the 1950s through the late '80s could very well have led to Hal's death and to his family's, as it did to many real people. For a fascinating account of Rocky Flats, written by a person who lived there, read *Full Body Burden: Growing Up in the Nuclear Shadow of Rocky Flats* by Kristen Iversen.

Clean up of Rocky Flats was not considered complete until October 13, 2005. The land is now Rocky Flats National Wildlife Refuge, a beautiful area 16 miles northwest of Denver. Federal, State, and local governments have declared it perfectly safe. Environmentalists have concerns. You decide if it's a place you'd like to visit.

An Updated Account of the Real Places Mentioned in
IT'S PERFECTLY SAFE...

If you, the reader, ever have a chance to visit Colorado, you are certain to travel along Interstate Highway 70, running clear across the state. Perhaps you'll stop at these interesting places, or at least recognize them from the road signs:

<u>Glenwood Canyon</u>: A spectacular twelve and one-half mile canyon, along the Colorado River, just east of the town of Glenwood Springs, formed by the river cutting through layers of bright red sandstone. You might like to get out of the car and hike to Hanging Lake or join one of the groups of whitewater rafters. When Todd drove through, Interstate 70 had not been built, so he would have had a difficult drive indeed, especially when someone tried to push him off the road. Meg rode the Vista Dome train from Denver. That is another way you could see this not widely known, stunning site.

<u>Glenwood Springs</u>: The largest town in Garfield County. You'll want to park and walk around. The traffic is dreadful, but it's a beautiful community, surrounded by red sandstone cliffs, and is best known for its hot sulphur springs and heated outdoor swimming pool. The water is fine—although smelly—even in the wintertime. President Franklin Roosevelt used to swim in the pool to help him in his battle against polio. Meg was unhappy because she was never allowed to swim as a child *because* of the polio scare. The author of *It's Perfectly Safe...* had the same experience.

<u>Rifle</u>: A good-sized town with lots to do. Most people are taken aback by the name. According to legend, a trapper in the late 19th century accidentally left his rifle along the creek and, well, the town needed a name. The author attended school and church in Rifle. If you visit the museum, you'll see aerial photos taken by her father, Ted Moore, back in the 1940s.

Rifle Falls State Park: Beautiful and worth the side trip you'll take from Rifle. You'll gasp at the triple 70-foot waterfall and, if you're slim, enjoy squeezing into some of the many narrow caves.

Anvil Points: Once a bustling mining community of 70 families, Anvil Points is now deserted and is being used for landfill and toxic waste. But it has a view that can't be beat. Be on the lookout for snakes, but do enjoy searching for fossils and interesting rocks. Anvil Points is not accessible from Interstate 70. You'll need to backtrack and take Route 6 out of Parachute. Both the author and the fictional Meg have wonderful memories of Anvil Points.

Parachute (Grand Valley): The residents are proud of the name, the only town named Parachute in the world. The name derived from the Ute word "Pahchou," meaning "twins," referring to the mountains on either side of the stream. Settlers mispronouncing the word re-christened it Parachute. In 1904, the town's name was changed to Grand Valley in the mistaken belief it would attract real estate investors. In 1980, the town became Parachute once again. It's a small, friendly community, with residents who are proud of their town and its history. Be looking for a one-story building with a teepee on top. Great gift store! And take the access road, Route 6, for a short trip east to Anvil Points.

Rulison: An unincorporated, tiny community 1.4 miles SW of Anvil Points and 6.7 miles from Parachute. Located on Route 70, not much is there—not even the general store the author's family often frequented. Rulison's main claim to fame today is Project Rulison.

Rulison Nuclear Blast Site: The address? Unnamed Rd., Parachute, CO. These are the directions given on Roadside America's guide to Offbeat Tourist Attractions: *I-70 exit 75. Drive south on CR 215/CR 300 for a half-mile, then bear left onto CR 301/N. Battlement Pkwy. Follow for a little over three miles (be careful to follow N. Battlement Pkwy, not E. Battlement Pkwy); then turn right onto CR 310. Follow until it dead-ends (around a mile), then make a sharp right onto an unnamed road and follow for around three miles. Stay straight when the road turns sharply left. Drive another thousand feet and look for the bright yellow Nuclear Blast Site sign behind the wooden fence.* It still sounds secretive, doesn't it? But if you've read this book and are in the area, you really should visit. The shaft has been sealed with cement, and a concrete plaque marks the spot where Meg's Skinny Boy "was planted." Do visit, but perhaps you shouldn't stay too long.

Battlement Mesa: Named for the surrounding geographic formations that resemble ancient fortresses, the community was created for oil shale employees by Exxon during the 1970s. When Exxon pulled out—a move that devastated Grand Junction and other towns—Battlement Mesa became a ghost town. It is now thriving and is one of the few planned communities in the state. From I-70, turn south, cross the Colorado River to the Battlement Mesa entrance.

Grand Junction: The largest town in Mesa County, located at the junction of the Colorado and Gunnison Rivers. GJ is famous for its peach crop, winery, and Mesa University. It's a biking destination and bikers come from around the world to partake of the excellent single-track trails. Those looking for beautiful scenery will enjoy the Colorado National Monument, the Grand Mesa, and the same Book Cliffs that are so much a part of Parachute. Places mentioned in the novel—Walker Field Airport, Horizon Drive, and St. Mary's Hospital—are all located in Grand Junction.

Marilyn and her mother Lillian Moore checking progress of Anvil Points home construction

Marilyn and her dog Pal in front of Big Boy Mountain

About the Author

MARILYN LUDWIG TEACHES THEATRE TO middle grade and high school students and has written many of the plays her students have performed. She is active in community theatre productions and has worked with numerous groups of youth at her church. She is a member of the Society of Children's Book Writers and Illustrators.

Marilyn was a child in the mining community of Anvil Points, where her father was employed as a civil engineer. Although the site has been closed for years, the mighty peaks remain, and she returns often to visit.

Other novels include *Searching for Juliette*, *Haste Ye Back*, and *The Secret of Kendall Mountain*. At present, she is working on a novel, taking place in wartime Bletchley Park, England.

www.ingramcontent.com/pod-product-compliance
Lightning Source LLC
Chambersburg PA
CBHW021127300426
44113CB00006B/324